READ TO ME

Gloria Rolton

Illustrated by Michelle Katsouranis

ACER
PRESS

First published 2001
by Australian Council for Educational Research Ltd
19 Prospect Hill Road, Camberwell, Melbourne, Victoria, 3124

1 3 5 7 9 10 8 6 4 2

Edited by Adrienne de Kretser, Righting Writing
Illustrated by Michelle Katsouranis
Cover and text design by Scooter Design
Typeset in 13.5/19 Perpetua by Scooter Design
Printed by Brown Prior Anderson

National Library of Australia Cataloguing-in-Publication data:

Rolton, Gloria.
Read to me.

Bibliography.
ISBN 0 86431 391 8.

1. Children - Australia - Books and reading. 2. Children's
literature - Australia - Bibliography. 3. Children - Language.
I. Katsouranis, Michelle. II. Title.

028.5

Visit our website: www.acerpress.com.au

Contents

Introduction

I hope this book helps you to experience the delight that can come from sharing books with your pre-schoolers. It is the result of my experiences in bringing children and books together over more than thirty years. I began sharing books with primary school children but in recent years have worked with three and four-year-olds through a weekly storybook session.

As a teacher in the late 1960s, I read to my class regularly. I knew they enjoyed it as we laughed together over such books as *Muddle-headed Wombat* or cried together over *Storm Boy*. I believed that this shared reading helped children to have a better understanding of how language worked. And it allowed me to introduce good books to developing readers who were not yet able to read them for themselves. Some twenty years later when I read of research in the United States that showed how children who were read to on a daily basis made great gains in a number of reading areas, I felt like cheering.

In the 1980s, the reading programs in South Australian schools moved from using the old style readers and reading laboratories to using real storybooks and novels. Reading to children was an important component of this approach. At my school I often spoke to groups of parents about their role in reading to their school-age children. As part of this talk, I read the parents a story. I usually chose *Alexander and the terrible, horrible, no good, very bad day*. The parents loved it and there was usually a number who asked to borrow the book. I pointed out that just as they enjoyed hearing a good story, so did their children, especially if it meant having Dad or Mum's total attention. Many of those parents came back to tell me they were reading to their children and how much they were enjoying it. I believed then as I do now that parents reading to children is vital. Most kids eventually learn to read but not all turn to reading for pleasure. It is parents who can change this so that those who can read become those who do read.

It was the arrival of my grandchildren that gave me

the opportunity to extend my ideas about reading to a younger audience. I began to put into practice the ideas that I had read about in Dorothy Butler's *Babies Need Books*. To see these little ones enjoying picture books and demanding their favourite stories even before they had fluent language was wonderful. From infancy they had access to good picture books and adults to share the wonder of books with them. My son-in-law was sceptical at first but was soon converted, especially when he saw his tiny daughter responding to an Anthony Browne book. Although he did comment once that if he had to read *Mr Magnolia* yet again, the book might come to grief!

My youngest grandchild, Kane, is just two-and-a-half years old. Recently we videotaped him with *Hairy Maclary from Donaldson's Dairy*. He loves this and has learned the text of the whole book. He sits and turns the pages and 'reads' it. Already he understands that the story has a beginning and an end and that it flows from page to page. From the illustrations he knows the different doggy characters and relishes the climax where 'Scarface Claw, the toughest tom in town' scares all the dogs and has them running off home. Like his brother and his older cousins, he will have no fear of learning to read when he begins school. It is possible that like his cousin Taylor he will be reading before he starts school.

But helping with early reading is just one of the advantages that reading to toddlers brings. In this book I have outlined a number of advantages. However, the most important reason for sharing books with your baby, toddler or pre-schooler should always be pleasure. If you and your child enjoy sharing a book then the other benefits will follow.

Gloria Rolton

The Value of Books
for Babies to Preschoolers

$\mathcal{A}$s the parent of a preschooler you are the single most important influence on your child and how they will develop. At no other time in their life will you have such a pivotal role. In these few years your child will learn to walk, talk and do all the physical things that humans are programmed to do. But through you they will learn the things that are not preprogrammed. This learning can happen as you play, tell stories and share books with your child.

Reading books and stories to children is fun for both adult and child. The time of closeness with a small child, sharing a picture book, a nursery rhyme book or telling a story builds a bond between parent and child.

Finding time to read can be a problem. Despite all the

gadgetry in modern homes, parents today are as busy as those of forty or fifty years ago. Many parents make a set time to read, such as at bedtime. Others use 'waiting' time – time spent waiting for an older child to finish music/ballet/sport/school. Dorothy Butler in *Babies Need Books* suggests a mid-morning break for shared reading. This may seem impossible for young mothers surrounded by the morning's clutter. But those of us with older children know these early years fly. Once they've passed for your child, they cannot be recaptured. And this time of sharing is vitally important for the preschool child to develop:

- language skills
- listening skills
- social skills
- cognitive skills (thinking, remembering and associating skills)
- problem-solving skills
- early reading skills.

LANGUAGE DEVELOPMENT

The basis for language begins in the first hours and days of your baby's life. As you talk to your child, baby begins to recognise your voice. From their first days your infant is hearing the rhythm of the parents' language. During the first year it will move from cooing to babbling. At this time children begin to imitate the sounds of the language about them and fit these to the rhythms that have become familiar. By singing songs, sharing rhymes and telling stories to your child you are providing the groundwork for language to develop.

The vocabulary of toddlers grows rapidly. Books and stories can help by providing a model. For example, before she was three Brittany was read *Rosie's Walk* by Pat Hutchins many times, but she had never seen a haystack such as the one that saves Rosie from the fox. However, when she saw a huge stack of drying garden cuttings she pointed to them and exclaimed, 'Look! A haystack!' She was experimenting with a word she had met only in a picture book. Children who experience good books will be exposed to more complex language. In *Peter Rabbit* children learn that Peter is caught by his jacket in Mr McGregor's garden and then 'his sobs were overheard by some friendly sparrows, who flew to him in great excitement and implored him to exert himself'.

LISTENING SKILLS

In their early years much of what children learn comes through listening. They need to develop the ability to listen, as distinct from hearing. If this seems odd, think of a recent news broadcast you sat through. You probably *heard* the voice droning on but were not really *listening* unless something caught your attention.

Many young children have learnt to 'turn off' sounds around them. This may be because television has become background noise in the home or because the child is 'talked at' rather than 'talked with'. I recently observed a family of mother, grandmother and three children eating out. The youngest child of about four wandered around; he would not sit and eat his meal. His mother kept up a continuous commentary aimed at him. His sister who sat and ate quietly was ignored. The disobedient one ignored his mother. He let her voice wash over him completely – it had become part of the background noise. The mother may have changed his listening behaviour if she had rewarded the sister for behaving so well. The four-year-old may have changed from 'hearing' to 'listening'.

Sharing story books is a fun way to help develop your toddler's listening skills. After reading a book, encourage the child to discuss the story. This may simply mean going back over the book and inviting them to comment on the illustrations. Often the toddler demands, 'Read it again'.

Encouraging your four-year-old to listen for longer

periods will help in their early days at school, when most information is given verbally. Listening to television is no substitute for a story from a real live adult who can read and hold a toddler on their lap at the same time. During story-reading most children assume an amazing amount of control, as they interrupt to comment or ask questions.

Sometimes the questions that arise while reading a picture book may force parents to check with a reference book. Remember the craze to know the names of all the different dinosaurs? This is an excellent opportunity for the preschooler to see that there are books for finding answers and that adults use them. If your family regularly uses a library, borrow a few factual books as well as story books. These may be on subjects that your child already enjoys or may introduce new wonders to them.

SOCIAL SKILLS

The family is every child's first social group. Later this will expand as they move to creche, kindergarten or school. As infants hear nursery rhymes, songs and stories from a parent or grandparent they are developing the sense that their place in the family social group is valued.

When they are read to they learn to make and maintain eye contact with the adult, which is an important feature of communication in our society. There is often an exchange of smiles, which is an introduction to the whole complicated business of human expressions and what they mean. By the time they are in their first years of school, children can judge facial expressions. Very quickly they are able to distinguish between a smile that is a real smile and one that is merely polite. They can soon judge the feelings of those in their social group by their facial expressions.

COGNITIVE DEVELOPMENT

The development of thinking, remembering and understanding is basic to learning. From the first year of a baby's life we play games such as 'This little piggy' and even the youngest child soon learns that the game ends in tickling. They are developing understanding by associating the rhyme and the accompanying actions.

Young children who are read to, soon have favourite books. Remembering the story, the book from which it came and favourite illustrations show that the child's cognitive skills are developing. These skills develop further with stories that show cause and effect.

When Jackson was two and a half he particularly liked *Watch Me* by Pamela Allen. This wordless book shows a small boy undertaking increasingly daring exploits on his three-wheeled bike then coming to grief. Although Jackson had 'read' it dozens of times, he gave a commentary each time: 'Naughty boy, not holding on, naughty boy! His knee bleeding'. When he wanted the book he always asked for the 'Naughty boy book'. His enjoyment of this small book reflected the development of his thinking skills, remembering skills and understanding of cause and effect.

PROBLEM-SOLVING SKILLS

Very young children have inquiring minds. You will have noticed that they seem to be continually asking 'Why?'.

Encouraging children to ask questions and find answers can help develop problem-solving skills, particularly if they can look at more than one possible solution to a problem.

We can encourage this through sharing picture books. When I read *Alexander's Outing* by Pamela Allen to Thomas, aged four and a half, I was surprised at his ability to understand the solution to Alexander's difficulty. The story shows a mother duck taking her brood of ducklings for a walk and one, Alexander, falls into a deep narrow hole. Several attempts are made to get Alexander out of the hole before someone begins to pour water into it. I asked Thomas why they were doing this and he explained it was so Alexander could swim to the top.

Especially good for allowing young readers to suggest a solution is Shirley Hughes' *Alfie Gets in First*. When Alfie slams the door he is locked inside the house with the shopping and Mum's keys; Mum is locked out. As several neighbours, the milkman and the window-cleaner offer advice Alfie solves the problem. Most young readers, when asked to suggest what Alfie should do, arrive at the same answer as Alfie. Allowing children to predict possible solutions to the problem faced by a character in a picture book helps develop problem-solving skills.

Older children may think of several solutions and select the best. This is valuable training for school, where several curriculum areas are based on children discovering answers to their problems.

E A R L Y   R E A D I N G

Children who are surrounded with books from babyhood, told stories and read to are greatly advantaged when they begin the task of learning to read. They expect that books will be enjoyable and they understand that the marks on the page can tell a story.

They are aware of how books work. They know that books read from front to back, from top to bottom and from left to right. These concepts are learnt unconsciously through sharing books. In homes where reading is a normal, everyday activity and shared with even the youngest there will be little or no fear of learning to read. It is seen as something that will happen as a matter of course because everyone at home does it.

Jim Trelease, in *The New Read Aloud Handbook*, cites a study of children who learnt to read earlier than their peers. It showed that all the early readers had been read to on a regular basis. Trelease claims that reading to preschool children 'stimulates their imagination, stretches

their attention span and improves their listening comprehension'. Such children enter their first year of school
greatly advantaged.

Ages and Stages
in Development

$\mathcal{A}$t some time we have all held a newborn baby and looked in wonder at this new being. There is an immense sense of responsibility for the vulnerability of this small person. But as the months pass we cannot help but be impressed by the changes that take place as the child shows an ability to adapt and to learn. This development occurs in the physical control that the baby gains over its body and in the understanding and development of language.

From the time they are a few hours old babies are smiled at, spoken and sung to. No one believes that the child can understand this early communication but that does not stop parents, other family members and carers from continuing the one-way conversation. Within only a few weeks, however, the baby is showing interest in voices and responding in small ways.

We know that early communication is important in helping baby and parents to bond, but it is also a very important part of the child's overall development. The following very brief examination of the different stages of child development can be useful. Parents who are aware of these stages can help their infant by knowing what activities, play and books fit the stage their child is reaching.

The first column of the table shows some of the developmental stages that children pass through. The second column suggests ways in which parents can help at that stage. However, you must remember that every child reaches the stages according to their own timetable and that those suggested here are only approximate. The third column gives book titles that can be used to help that stage of development.

This table suggests books that will help children at the different stages of their development. These are just a few of the many books that are available. The following chapters give detailed lists of books that may be available in your local library or through bookshops.

Note: 'OP' indicates that the book is no longer in print and you won't find it in a bookshop. It may, however, be available in your library.

DEVELOPMENTAL STAGES

CHARACTERISTICS OF THE CHILD	ACTION REQUIRED OF THE CARER	APPROPRIATE BOOKS
0–12 months	0–12 months	0–12 months
At about 3 months begins to respond with pleasure to friendly handling	Maintain eye contact and use songs and rhymes	*This Little Puffin* compiled by Elizabeth Matterson
Visually very alert, uses eyes to follow objects	Provide brightly coloured and uncluttered pictures	Dick Bruna books of single objects
At about 6 months laughs and squeals in play	Fingerplays and rhymes	*Baby Games* by Elaine Martin
Uses whole hand to grasp objects	Share small, sturdy board books	*Spot at the Farm* by Eric Hill

CHARACTERISTICS OF THE CHILD	ACTION REQUIRED OF THE CARER	APPROPRIATE BOOKS
0–12 months	**0–12 months**	**0–12 months**
Child's babbling imitates the intonation of speech in the home	Model normal speech. Continue with songs, games and rhymes	Books of nursery rhymes
Begins grasping with thumb and fingers	Provide small board books that the child can hold and handle	*Bumping and Bouncing* by Alison Lester, board books
After 12 months first word names (nouns)	Provide books showing objects that are suitable for pointing at and naming	*Babytime ABC*, *Babytime 123* (Brown Watson)
12–24 months	**12–24 months**	**12–24 months**
Understands many of the words that are spoken to them and uses some words	Books showing familiar events and happenings	*Bibs and Boots* by Alison Lester, board books
Begins to use pincer grip to pick up objects	Provide sturdy-page story books showing familiar events	Bob Graham books
Curious about people and objects in their world	Stories of children, family and the home	*Alfie's Feet* by Shirley Hughes
By 18 months the child can understand much of the language of home	Provide books to extend language and experiences	*When We Play Together* by Nick Butterworth
Imitates and repeats words	Provide books that are fun and allow the child to play with words and sounds	*Hairy Maclary* by Linley Dodd

Characteristics of the child	Action required of the carer	Appropriate books
12–24 months	**12–24 months**	**12–24 months**
Rapid spurt in language by 2 years	Allow for wide range of subjects in stories and books	Mog stories by Judith Kerr
2–3 years	**2–3 years**	**2–3 years**
The child is the centre of their world	Provide stories and books that reflect the child's world	*Can't You Sleep, Little Bear?* by Martin Waddell
Short attention span	Use books that feature familiar events	*Has Anyone Here Seen William?* by Bob Graham
Rapid language growth	Provide books to extend the child's experiences	*Very Hungry Caterpillar* by Eric Carle
Manual dexterity is being refined	Child enjoys using books that can be manipulated	*Where's Spot?* by Eric Hill
The child understands the concept of imaginary play	Allow stories and books that show the child in real and imaginary situations	*We're Going on a Bear Hunt* illustrated by Helen Oxenbury
3–4 years	**3–4 years**	**3–4 years**
Developing understanding of how things relate to each other	Provide stories that show cause and effect	*Alexander's Outing* by Pamela Allen
Building concepts such as colour, shape, number and size	Allow for play to extend and develop these concepts	*But Where is the Green Parrot?* by Thomas Zacharias

CHARACTERISTICS OF THE CHILD	ACTION REQUIRED OF THE CARER	APPROPRIATE BOOKS
3–4 years	**3–4 years**	**3–4 years**
Speech involves more complex use of adverbs, adjectives and pronouns	Books and stories should allow for the child's vocabulary to be extended	*Rosie's Walk* by Pat Hutchins
Involved in 'make-believe' play	Encourage the use of imagination and make-believe	*There's a Hippopotamus on the Roof Eating Cake* by Hazel Edwards
Attention span is longer	Read and tell longer stories	*Arthur* by Amanda Graham
Understands sharing	Provide books that show children at play	*I Wish I had a Pirate Suit* by Pamela Allen
Develops a sense of humour	Find books that allow for fun and nonsense	*Mr Magnolia* by Quentin Blake
Understands past, present and future	Introduce books and stories that show passage of time	*The Bad-tempered Ladybird* by Eric Carle
Good physical control of hands and fingers	Allow for manipulative skills by using flap books	*Mog and Barnaby* by Judith Kerr
Needs companionship of other children	Play groups or creche	*Mum Goes to Work* by Libby Gleeson
Learns that other children may differ in looks	Provide stories and books that show children from other cultures	*Cleversticks* by Bernard Ashley

Note: The format of this chart is based on Donna Norton, *Through the Eyes of a Child: An Introduction to Children's Literature,* Merrill Publishing, 1983.

Fingerplays,

Action Rhymes

and Singing Games

*T*raditional songs and games are used in families from one generation to the next. The finger games you play with your child may be those your parents or grandparents played with you. What value is there in sharing these with infants and toddlers?

The first value, of course, is enjoyment. Those of us who have played 'Round and round the garden' or 'This little piggy went to market' with a small child and witnessed the giggling delight of the infant who knows that the rhyme ends with tickling, also know that the fun is shared by the adult. But in addition to enjoyment your infant is being helped in:

- social development
- physical development

- cognitive development
- language development.

SOCIAL DEVELOPMENT

It is important for the infant to mature and take their place in first the family and then the larger community. Early games offer an enjoyable interaction with the people who form the child's first community. During this play the baby learns to make and maintain eye contact with a carer and to exchange smiles.

Newspapers some years ago featured photographs of babies in countries that were formerly behind the Iron Curtain. These babies and toddlers, unwanted because they were the children of AIDS patients, sat in hospital cots unaware of the events around them. They had not learnt to make eye contact or to respond to smiles. The children had been denied the attention that most babies are given and this showed in their failure to develop the normal social skills of infants.

PHYSICAL DEVELOPMENT

This is aided through finger plays and action rhymes. Very early games draw attention to different body parts. As we recite 'This little piggy' we touch the child's toes. During another rhyme we lightly touch their forehead, eyes, nose, lips and chin. As they grow, play becomes more active and we encourage them to ride astride a knee or jog on a suspended foot as we sing 'Ride a cock-horse'. By taking part in these games the child is developing co-ordination of small and large body movements, as well as hand–eye co-ordination. This co-ordination is important preparation for sitting, crawling, walking and the many other actions that require different body parts to work together. As children are introduced to finger plays such as 'Incy wincy spider' they need a degree of control over their fingers. This control is important later as they learn to feed themselves, dress and use pencils, paints and scissors in kindergarten and school.

COGNITIVE DEVELOPMENT

The children's thinking, remembering and understanding is helped as they hear rhymes and, over time, learn to associate the correct movements of each. After several games of 'Round and round the garden' the infant knows what to expect and begins to draw away to make it more difficult for the adult to tickle under their arm. Children are much quicker at forming these associations than we give them credit for. For example, when Ebony was a toddler it was sometimes difficult to get her to sleep. I had, without realising it, always sung the nursery song 'Hey-de, hey-de ho, the great big elephant is so slow' as I rocked her to sleep. But she was well aware of the association, and on one occasion when she had no intention of sleeping said very clearly 'No hey-de ho!'.

LANGUAGE DEVELOPMENT

Songs, fingerplays and action rhymes play an important role in the child's ability to develop language. We know that the groundwork for language development begins in the first hours and days of a baby's life. As you talk and sing to your child you are introducing them not only to the comfort and security of being held, but to the comfort of your voice. Young babies can soon recognise their mother's voice as distinct from other female voices.

It may appear that your child in the first months is doing nothing towards learning language, but they are in fact learning very actively. During their first year, babies begin to imitate the sounds of language around them and to fit these into the rhythms they have become familiar with. At birth, children can produce the sounds for all human languages but they gradually cease making the sounds that are not part of their environment. In the pre-speaking stage, as they begin to babble, many toddlers use inflections that so closely imitate language they often sound like statements and questions.

By singing songs and sharing rhymes and fingerplays you are providing models to help your child learn the rhythm and sounds of their language.

BOOKS TO LOOK FOR

While many of the traditional songs and fingerplays can be dredged up from your memory, there are some books that are particularly helpful. The larger and more expensive collections may be available at your local library.

Action Songs, compiled by Helen Finnigan, illustrated by Roger Langton (Ladybird Books, OP). This little

book, and its companions *Counting Songs, First Songs*
and *Finger Rhymes*, may be available at your library. It
has fifteen songs with the actions for each, including
such songs as 'If you're happy and you know it, clap
your hands' and 'Old McDonald'.

Clap Your Hands: finger rhymes chosen by Sarah Hayes
(Walker). This is a collection of twenty-four popular
rhymes to share with infants and toddlers. It includes
'Here is the beehive', 'Incy wincy spider' and 'Five fat
peas'.

Dancing and Singing Games, selected by Pie Corbett
and Sally Emerson, illustrated by Moira and Colin
Maclean (Kingfisher Nursery Library, OP). You may
remember many of the twenty-five singing games
included in this paperback, such as 'Here we go round
the mulberry bush', 'Oranges and lemons' and 'The
big ship sails on the alley, alley O'.

Hand Rhymes, by Marc Brown (Collins). This author
has produced a series of books that are very useful.
Look for *Play Rhymes, Party Rhymes* and *Finger Rhymes*.
Both words and actions are shown.

*Little Billy Bandicoot: Rhymes and Songs for Australian
Children*, by Jean Chapman, illustrated by Sandra

Laroche (Lothian Books). This is a large hardback book that contains traditional fingerplays, hand games, songs and much, much more. Jean Chapman's collections are well-known in schools but this is great for the home. Each section begins with advice from an author who knows children and their interests. The illustrations are delightful.

Play Rhymes, collected and illustrated by Marc Brown (Collins). These twelve rhymes are illustrated beautifully in soft tones, each on a double-page spread. The actions are shown in a small square at the start of each line.

Ring O' Roses: Nursery Rhymes, Action Rhymes and Lullabies, illustrated by Priscilla Lamont (Angus & Robertson, OP). This beautifully illustrated book may be available from your library. It is certainly worth checking. It has such fingerplays as 'Round and round the garden' and 'Pat-a-cake', along with 'Jack and Jill', 'Little Miss Muffett' and some beautiful lullabies. The music for the lullabies is also given.

Round and Round the Garden, by Sarah Williams, illustrated by Ian Beck (Oxford University Press). This is a delight. There are forty finger or play rhymes, each beautifully illustrated. The finger or hand actions are shown in sketches along the bottom of each page. Favourites such as 'Incy wincy spider', 'I'm a little teapot' and 'Five fat sausages' are included.

Round and Round the Garden and Other Hand Rhymes, illustrated by Louise Comfort (Walker). This is great. Each rhyme is illustrated, and a multiracial group of children demonstrate the actions.

This Little Puffin: Nursery Songs and Rhymes, compiled by Elizabeth Matterson (Puffin). This is a handy paperback that can be useful for many years. Many of the songs are ones that children learn in kindergarten or even in junior primary school. The actions for fingerplays are shown.

A search of your local library will unearth many other titles that are no longer in print or not available locally. One such title is *I'll Tell You a Story, I'll Sing you a Song: A Parents' Guide to the Fairy Tales, Fables, Songs and Rhymes of Childhood* by Christine Allison (Delacorte Press). This volume of more than 200 pages is organised into seven sections and covers the stories, songs and rhymes that parents may have forgotten. It's a great resource.

Nursery Rhymes

Many of the nursery rhymes that we share with our children are very old. Donna Norton, in *Through the Eyes of a Child*, tells of the origin of such rhymes as 'Old King Cole', 'Little Jack Horner' and 'Humpty Dumpty'. She links them to English royalty and the English court of the past. When we think about the fate of those who opposed such powerful individuals as Henry VIII it is understandable that critics might camouflage their views in what appeared to be nonsense verse.

THEIR VALUE TO INFANTS

Nursery rhymes have been a family tradition for many generations. Even before parents read to their children they were able to share these rhymes. The meaning of some rhymes is obscure but this does not lessen the fun of sharing. Parents and grandparents are delighted when a toddler first manages to sing along with 'Baa, baa black sheep' or 'Twinkle, twinkle little star'.

In discussing nursery rhymes, Dorothy Butler points out that 'They are part of our children's heritage, in an age when too little is handed down. There is a world of security and satisfaction in knowing children don't really change from generation to generation; that some of the best things are still the oldest'.

But awareness of our heritage is not the only reason for using nursery rhymes with infants. Nursery rhymes help children in the following areas:

- social development
- language development
- cognitive development
- reading development.

SOCIAL DEVELOPMENT

Children first learn how social groups work within the informal setting of their family. Many social problems that develop with older children are said to come from low self-esteem. In these early years, talking with and listening to your child builds the sense that they are valued. Sharing nursery rhymes is an enjoyable way to continue this.

After this period children move to social groups out-side the family: either creche or kindergarten. Finding that nursery rhymes from home are part of the new group's activities gives a sense of familiarity. It provides a common ground to help children 'fit in' and feel part of the new group.

LANGUAGE DEVELOPMENT

Nursery rhymes also have an important role in the child's language development. The greatest growth in language occurs between two and six years. Toddlers and preschool children delight in playing with the rhythm and sound of language. I can remember one of my sons discovering rhyming: he wandered around chanting 'Tony – pony – wony – rony – fony'. His enjoyment appeared to be through the 'feel' of the sounds, nothing to do with mak-ing any meaning. By using nursery rhymes with children at this stage we are encouraging them to practise and enjoy rhythm and rhyme.

Nursery rhymes allow a story to unfold – their story is developed often within just four lines! So, well before they have fluent language skills, infants and toddlers are being introduced to story. And story is basic to our language: we use the 'story form' to communicate with people around us. Think how often we greet those we haven't seen for some time by saying 'I must tell you about...' or 'Have you heard...?'.

COGNITIVE DEVELOPMENT

From their first years children's cognitive skills (thinking, remembering and forming associations) are developing. Remembering nursery rhymes and associating illustrations with the rhymes is one indication of this. Brittany especially liked the *Hilda Boswell Treasury of Nursery Rhymes* at about two and half, and always wanted to turn to 'Polly put the kettle on'. She not only remembered the rhyme but knew the page because of the illustration.

Another way in which the cognitive aspects are reinforced is through rhymes that shows cause and effect. From a very early stage children see that if 'this' happens then 'that' follows. There is a recognition of good and evil – albeit a very simple kind of good and evil – in such rhymes as 'Ding dong dell' and 'There was a little girl'.

EARLY READING

Being familiar with nursery rhymes will help in the early years of school when children are beginning to read.

Many of the Big Books used for shared reading in the first years of school involve nursery rhymes. Children who are familiar with nursery rhymes find Big Books much easier than those who are not. They already know the words of the rhyme and the meaning, so they only have to learn what the words look like on a Big Book page.

HOW TO SELECT BOOKS

Many outstanding illustrators have recently produced nursery rhyme collections. It is interesting to look at the different styles of illustration. For many years nursery rhyme books showed children wearing sixteenth or seventeenth-century clothes. Today they may show children of different ethnic backgrounds, just as happens in the creche or kindergarten where children are using the books.

When choosing a nursery rhyme collection, look at several of the rhymes that have been your favourites. Check to see that the words are those you are familiar with, then check the illustrations. We all enjoy different styles of illustration and these books will be read many many times, so ensure the style is one you will still enjoy when you are reading it for the twentieth or thirtieth time! One way to sample them is to seek the different collections at your local library or bookshop. The library may have some of the collections that, unfortunately, are no longer in print.

As well as large nursery rhyme books to share with a child on your knee, don't overlook pocket-sized books that can be a great diversion when waiting in the car, at the doctor or other places when toddlers become restless. I've found a small book of nursery rhymes to be a great standby when taking a toddler to visit Mum in hospital where everyone is making a fuss of the new baby sister or brother!

BOOKS TO LOOK FOR

The following are collections, both old and new, that you might like to share with your infants and toddlers.

ABC Book of Nursery Rhymes (ABC). All the old

favourites are included in this large-size book. The illustrations by some of Australia's outstanding illustrators show a variety of styles.

A Child's Treasury of Nursery Rhymes, illustrated by Kady Macdonald Denton (Kingfisher). This large book is divided into four sections: 'Welcome Little Baby', 'Toddler Time', 'In the Schoolyard' and 'All Join In'. It has all the old favourites and some that are less familiar.

A Day of Rhymes, selected and illustrated by Sarah Pooley (Random). This collection will take toddler and adult through the whole day from waking until bedtime, with more than sixty rhymes to share. The illustrations show fathers as well as mothers with their children.

A First Picture Book of Nursery Rhymes, illustrated by Elizabeth Harbour (Puffin). Gently illustrated, this slim paperback has twenty-eight well-known rhymes.

Bedtime Rhymes (Ladybird). This small and inexpensive book has soft illustrations that match the gentle tones of the rhymes. A great standby for bedtime.

Classic Nursery Rhymes, illustrated by Tracey Moroney

(Five Mile Press). Here are all the well-known rhymes. The illustrations are large and colourful. Each page has a coloured border that gives an appealing nostalgic look.

Collins Book of Nursery Rhymes, illustrated by Jonathan Langley (HarperCollins). This is a beautifully presented collection in hardback that will last many years as a family treasure. See also *Favourite Nursery Rhymes* by the same illustrator.

For Teddy and Me: A Collection of Nursery Rhymes, chosen and illustrated by Pru Theobalds (Lothian). This lovely collection of twenty-four rhymes all feature teddy bears in the illustrations.

Helen Oxenbury Nursery Rhyme Book, verses chosen by Brian Alderson, illustrated by Helen Oxenbury (Collins). This collection has some of the well-known rhymes such as 'Baa, baa, black sheep' and 'Little Polly Flinders', together with many that are less well-known. Helen Oxenbury's illustrations are fun.

Hickory Dickory Dock and Other Rhymes (Ladybird). This small and inexpensive volume is great to keep in the car. It contains twenty-eight rhymes that are great to share with a restless toddler. Others in the series are *Humpty Dumpty and Other Rhymes* and *Incy Wincy Spider*.

Hickory Dickory Dock, by Carol Jones (Angus & Robertson). This collection uses peepholes in the pages that allow the reader to anticipate what will come next. Eleven of the favourites such as 'Little Bo-peep' and 'Hey diddle diddle' are here, along with 'Hickory dickory dock'. Preschoolers and older children will enjoy looking for and finding the little mouse from the title rhyme on every page.

I See the Moon and the Moon Sees Me . . . Helen Craig's Book of Nursery Rhymes (Collins). This title is fifty pages packed with fun. The illustrations are a delight – even the contents page forms a simple rebus that children will enjoy. The detailed illustrations will intrigue both adults and children. My favourite is possibly the cross section that shows how the old woman who lived in a shoe managed to accommodate her family.

Jack and Jill: A Book of Nursery Rhymes, compiled by Gwenda Beed Davey, illustrated by Betina Ogden (Hodder & Stoughton). This is a collection of all the old favourites with a hint of an Australian background in the outstanding illustrations. These are full of action: Jack and Jill are shown with the pail of water in mid-fall and Miss Muffett really has had a fright.

Michael Foreman's Nursery Rhymes (Walker). While the rhymes are the well-known ones it is the soft water-colour illustrations that make this a truly memorable book. This is a collection to give as a gift to a special infant or to add to the family library.

Nicola Bayley's Book of Nursery Rhymes (Random). The very detailed illustrations in this are extremely beautiful and arranged with a sense of balance.

Nursery Rhymes, chosen by Ronne Randall, illustrated by Peter Stevenson (Ladybird). This large volume is divided into four sections: 'Nursery Rhymes', 'Playtime Rhymes', 'Number Rhymes' and 'Bedtime Rhymes'. The contents page lists the titles in each section. The illustrations, together with the arrangement, makes this a very attractive book. See also *Nursery Rhyme Collection Two*.

Nursery Rhymes for Young Australians, illustrated by Jan Wade (Child & Associates). There are only eighteen rhymes in this collection, but all are set firmly in Australia. Humpty Dumpty wears a checked bush shirt, a hat with corks around the brim and carries a black billy. He seems to have been startled by a kookaburra. Little Bo-peep wears a t-shirt with an Australian logo and is watched by galahs as she searches for her lost sheep.

Over the Hills and Far Away: A Book of Nursery Rhymes, selected and illustrated by Alan Marks (Picture Book Studio, OP). Like other books from this publisher, the illustrations are outstanding. Soft watercolours on quality paper make this a delightful collection.

Playtime Rhymes (Ladybird). This beautifully illustrated book contains thirty rhymes covering counting rhymes, fingerplays and other action games.

Board Books

$\mathcal{M}$any parents of young children prefer to buy copies of board books rather than use library books because at this early stage children put everything into their mouths. You will find these books are quite sturdy and will not be damaged by being wiped with a damp cloth if they do become grubby or chewed. Several of the board books in my collection have teeth marks left by young readers.

Their value to infants

The 'ages and stages' information shows times in your baby's development when board books are particularly valuable.

- When the child can focus on objects, board books such as Ladybird First Focus are especially useful.

The colours are bright and the objects shown are large, simple shapes often outlined in black against a contrasting background.

- When the grasping ability has developed, introduce small chunky books that the baby can hold. These too should depict single items in easily defined shapes and bright colour.

- When the baby begins to point at objects on the page (but does not have words for them) board books are excellent. Well before the child can speak, it is not uncommon to hear a parent asking, 'Show me the puppy' or 'Where is the ball?' and the baby pointing. This is an indication that the child's receptive language (the language they understand) is far ahead of their spoken language.

- As the baby first uses words, board books are useful to extend their early vocabulary. ABC books are valuable at this stage as each page shows a single item from the child's world.

- As their pincer grip develops, children can hold and manipulate books for themselves. This gives the mobile infant some control over the selection of books either to 'read' alone or to insist that others read to them.

- When toddlers show that they can understand

simple stories, board books will stand up to rough handling.

HOW TO SELECT BOOKS

- Look at the size and shape of the overall book. When a baby is at the early grasping stage the smaller size books are best. This allows them to hold the book without becoming frustrated.
- For the very young, ensure that the book corners are rounded. Quite often a child still gaining control of its hands brings the book close to the line of vision and on to its face.
- Look at the pictures. Are the colours bright and the shapes easily recognised? In the early stages illustrations are easier to identify than photographs since all unnecessary detail is left out.
- When babies are developing their first words, and again at the 'point and say' stage, books that show single items on an uncluttered page will be most helpful.
- As the child's receptive language (the language understood but not used) develops, board books should show everyday events in and around the home. Bob Graham, Alison Lester and Helen Oxenbury's books are excellent examples of simple everyday

events such as dressing, helping, playing or sleeping.

- There should be very simple text in board books. When the child can follow a longer story they are ready for sharing picture books.

BOOKS TO LOOK FOR

All About Baby (Penguin Snap Shots Padded Board Books). This has padded covers and is easy to grasp. The photographs are of babies and animals. Series titles include *Good Morning Baby*, *Baby and Friends* and *Good Night Baby*.

Baby Animals, by Rod Campbell (Campbell Books). Like other books by the same author, this is attractive to infants and toddlers. The baby animals are all shown with their mothers. The pages are very thick. See also *Zoo Animals*.

Bibs and Boots, by Alison Lester (Allen & Unwin). Alison Lester's Baby Books delight young toddlers as they show a family of three children and their normal daily routines. This title shows the children eating breakfast, playing in the garden, at a party, at the beach, splashing in the rain and finally going to bed. Other titles are *Bumping and Bouncing* and *Crashing and Splashing*.

Buster's Park, by Rod Campbell (Campbell Books/ Macmillan). In this little board book we join Buster in the park as he plays on a slide, pats a dog and plays with a ball. See also *Buster's Farm*.

Daisy's Day Out, by Jane Simmons (Orchard). This is a large-size board book featuring Daisy, the duckling that toddlers will meet again in their first picture books. There are lots of lovely sounds as we join Daisy on her walk. Another title to look for is *Daisy Says Coo!*

GRRRR! Who's in the Jungle? (Book Company). This title and its companion BAA! use flaps to conceal an animal. They are attractive and strongly constructed to withstand the wear they will obviously receive.

Home, by Pierre Pratt (Campbell Books). This is about Olaf the elephant and Venus the mouse. The child is introduced to the telephone, door, cheese and bath in Olaf's home. He uses the phone to invite Venus, opens the door to let her in and then entertains her. *Park*, *Shops* and *Car* are more stories about Olaf and Venus.

I Can, illustrated by Helen Oxenbury (Walker Board Books). All titles by this illustrator show real activi-

ties to which children can relate. In this the small toddler can crawl, bend, jump and stamp. Other titles in
the series are *I Touch* and *I See*.

I Won't Bite, by Rod Campbell (Campbell Books). This
has different textures on each page for the toddler to
explore. They range from the delicate softness of
a mouse's ear or a rabbit's tail to the roughness of a
crocodile's skin.

It's Mine, by Rod Campbell (Campbell Books/
Macmillan). On each page the young reader is
encouraged to guess who owns the body part being
shown. These range from a pink tongue or a long
nose to a green tail.

Let's Make a Noise, by Amy MacDonald & Maureen
Roffey (Walker Books). These square books are the
right size to be handled by infants. This book shows
the toddler experimenting with animal noises.
Other titles in the series are *Let's Do It*, *Let's Play* and
Let's Try.

Let's Go, by Caroline Ansley (Walker). This small,
chunky board book shows different forms of trans-
port. Other titles in the series are *My First Things*

with items that the toddler will recognise, and *Wild Animals*.

Little Duckling, by Nicola Smee (Orchard). We see Little Duckling hatching and follow his walk to the pond to join his mother and the other ducklings. Other titles to look for are *Little Chick*, *Little Piglet* and *Little Rabbit*.

Look, Touch and Feel with Buster, by Rod Campbell (Thomas Lothian). The small character of Buster is featured in other books by this author. In this title the reader is encouraged to investigate the pages by looking under curtains and feeling different fabrics and textures. Toddlers enjoy the fun.

Miffy Goes Visiting, by Dick Bruna (Methuen Children's Books). Miffy is the appealing little rabbit who has been popular with children for more than thirty years. Children will find Miffy again in easy-to-read first books.

Spot at the Farm, by Eric Hill (William Heinemann). In this small book Spot scampers around and introduces the young reader to a variety of farm animals. The books in this series are chunky board books and easily manipulated. The illustrations are clear against white backgrounds. Other titles include *Play with Spot*, *Spot in the Garden*, *Spot at the Fair*, and *Spot Looks at Opposites*.

Stroke Henry, by Rod Campbell (Campbell Books/ Macmillan). The young reader can touch different textures as Henry the dog comes across them in his playing. They can feel Henry's fur, a towel on the clothesline, and can lift a flap to let Henry into the garden or explore the gap in the fence through which Henry pushes.

ABC and Counting Books

Their value to infants

We do not use ABC and counting books with children before they start school with the aim of teaching toddlers to count or to know the alphabet. But they do provide simple, inexpensive material for helping the child's language, social and cognitive development.

Language development

With infants up to two years, the books are particularly helpful. Sturdy little ABC board books may be used when the child can focus on objects while Mum or Dad supplies the name. As the child's understanding of language develops, the interaction changes. The parent who used to point at the page and say 'Look at the puppy' can say instead 'Where is the puppy?', allowing the child to show that they understand the language even if they are not yet using it. As the child's vocabulary develops the parent may point at items and ask 'What is this?', allowing the infant to give the name.

ABC and counting books are valuable as a means of expanding the toddler's vocabulary. These books can introduce animals, household items, food and clothing that are not present in the child's immediate environment. Infants meet elephants, monkeys and giraffes in books before they visit the zoo. City children become aware of cows, sheep and horses before they see the real thing, and country children meet electric trains, trams and jets in a similar way.

COGNITIVE DEVELOPMENT

At the same time as the child is developing language their cognitive skills (skills in thinking, remembering and associating) are developing. Remembering and naming the objects in a book proves this. Some concepts are part of both language and cognitive development. As part of their cognitive development toddlers understand the idea that things they know can appear in different forms. They may be told that an illustration of a small black animal is a dog.

But they soon learn that 'dog' can also be a large white animal or the animal that comes bounding towards them in the street. This concept (that things which appear different may have the same name) can be reinforced by introducing books with different styles of illustration. The toddler who masters this concept demonstrates a degree of thinking, remembering and associating.

While using number books children may be introduced to the names of numbers well before they understand the concept of what constitutes a group of three, five or two. This early introduction may help later in seeing the connection between the number of things and the name; for example, two birds, three babies or four cats.

SOCIAL SKILLS

During this early interaction between child, parent and book, the child is being helped with their social skills.

- They learn that people in our society make and hold eye contact when they are speaking.
- They learn the simple conventions of conversation, such as questions and answers.
- During these times the child has the parent's total attention, which helps build self-esteem. It is important that children feel valued before they start kindergarten.

Many educators believe that low self-esteem is the reason why some children fail to learn at school.

- Self-esteem is strengthened when children's responses are greeted with enthusiasm.

How to select books

When choosing ABC and counting books for your child you should remember the following.

- Some attractive ABC and counting books are available in board books that are suitable for quite young infants.
- For very young children, the illustrations should be clear and uncluttered.
- For children aged twelve to eighteen months, look for ABC books with only one or two illustrations per page. This helps in developing visual discrimination, a skill that is very important later in learning to read. Illustrations in counting books should show easily identified objects.
- Look for illustrations that have clear outlines and bright colours rather than soft muted colours with undefined outlines.
- Illustrations are more easily identified by younger children if they appear against a white or neutral background.

- Some alphabet and counting books have flaps and tabs. These will be useful when toddlers are able to manipulate them.
- ABC books are more useful if the letters are shown in lower case rather than capitals. Many children are confused when they begin school if they have had contact with only capital letters at home.
- Older preschool children will enjoy the more complicated illustration styles in some ABC and counting books. *Animalia* (Graham Base) or *Anno's ABC* (Anno) reward the readers who spend time to look into them carefully.

ABC BOOKS TO LOOK FOR

ABC, by Jan Pienkowski (Reed Books). Pienkowski's books use simple outlines and brilliant colour to show objects. This title is a small, chunky board book.

Animal Capers, by Kerry Argent (Omnibus). Kerry Argent's Australian animals are a delight. This can be an introduction to the story books and flap books in which many of these characters reappear.

Gwenda Turner's Australian ABC (Puffin). The distinctly Australian illustrations in this book are very life-like.

Lucy and Tom's ABC, by Shirley Hughes (Puffin). Shirley Hughes' illustrations show that she understands children and their place in the family.

Maisy's ABC, by Lucy Cousins (Walker). There are several books about this little mouse and many children have met Maisy on television. Here she takes us through the alphabet.

One Day: A Very First Dictionary, by Ann James (Hodder & Stoughton). Although this is labelled as a dictionary it is in fact an alphabet book. It shows the events of a young toddler's day.

Quentin Blake's ABC, by Quentin Blake (Jonathan Cape). Blake's riotous illustrations show situations based on the different letters of the alphabet. Across the bottom of each page are sentences that form rhyming couplets and add to the fun of reading the book aloud.

Counting books to look for

1-2-3, by Gwenda Turner (Puffin). The numbers in this counting book show very life-like animals.

1 2 3, by Jan Pienkowski (Reed Books). This board book is in a small chunky format.

Bad Babies Counting Book, by Tony Bradman (Red Fox).

This is great from the start, with one bad baby bouncing on his bed. We meet other bad babies doing such
things as putting their breakfast on their heads, fight-
ing at creche or causing havoc in the bathroom.
Preschool children will love it.

One Woolly Wombat, by Rod Trinka, illustrated by Kerry
Argent (Omnibus). This counting book shows a number of Australian birds and animals enjoying
themselves. The illustrations show up clearly against
a white background.

Wordless Books

~~~~~~

Wordless books are great. They may be used with toddlers, older preschool or school-aged children. They are particularly helpful when children are developing language skills. A wordless book shows events in correct sequence and the child tells the 'story' to match. Three-year-olds in particular want to do things unaided – wordless books enable them to 'read' for themselves.

THEIR VALUE TO CHILDREN

One great advantage of wordless books is that they can be shared by children and parents who have English as a second language. Whatever language is spoken in the home, the story is available for the child and parent to share in the language they choose.

Wordless books allow children to develop their creativity. Although the illustrations are set, the children still have room to create their own story. The reader can give the illustrated children names, decide where the story is taking place, tell why the events are happening as they are and tell what happened after the book ends. After becoming familiar with commercial books, children can be helped to use family photographs or magazine illustrations to create their own wordless book.

Another value of these books is the understanding of sequence. *Sunshine* by Jan Ormerod shows, on one double-page spread, a series of twelve slices of time during which a small girl changes from night clothes to day clothes. Understanding sequence is vital for learning to read. When reading, children need to be able to predict what will come next to make sense of the text. And making sense of print is surely what we mean by 'reading'.

COGNITIVE ABILITY

Wordless books can help develop the cognitive ability of preschool children. The children are required to *think* if they are to construct the story from the illustrations. They must *understand* what is happening if they are to build it into a story and must *remember* if they are to reconstruct the story at the next reading. *Sunshine* and its companion book *Moonlight* by Jan Ormerod are two that I have used with three-year-olds. Morgan showed her understanding of the events connecting the two books when she commented that both books 'had the same Daddy in them'.

Watch Me by Pamela Allen is a small wordless book that allows children to see cause and effect as a young bicycle rider defies the rules of safety. Unfortunately, it is no longer in print but you may find a copy in your library.

OBSERVATION SKILLS

Children can use wordless books to develop their observation skills. Books such as *Window*, *Millicent* or *Where the Forest Meets the Sky* by Jeannie Baker are either wordless or have very little text. Yet each rewards the reader who examines them closely. Young children find all sorts of interesting things in the small backyard of *Window* and enjoy bringing them to the notice of adults.

Wordless picture books help to reinforce what are called 'book conventions'. To make sense of the 'story' the child must read the book from front to back, from the top of the page to the bottom and from left to right. This is logical to adults, who know how to read, but it is not always obvious to a toddler or preschool child. These conventions are reinforced as the child shares the book with an adult and 'reads' the story from the illustrations. This is particularly important for later success in learning to read.

HOW TO SELECT BOOKS

Care has to be taken when selecting wordless books for preschool children since not all books without words are for very young readers.

Donna Norton, in *Through the Eyes of a Child* (1983), details a number of points to keep in mind when selecting wordless books.

- There needs to be a well-organised, sequential plot that young children can follow.
- The detail should be appropriate for the age of the children – too much detail can be overwhelming for young readers.
- The size of the book and its overall appeal must be considered.
- The illustrations should show situations that the child can understand.

BOOKS TO LOOK FOR

Not all of these books are still in print but many can be found in public libraries.

A Day on the Avenue, by Robert Roenfeldt (Puffin). An engaging book portraying the events in one street from early morning until night. The people who live there are shown leaving for work, preparing for visitors and meeting delivery workers. The normal suburban events such as garbage collection and postal deliveries are shown and preschoolers can relate to them.

Changes Changes, by Pat Hutchins (Red Fox). These illustrations depict a group of building blocks arranged and rearranged by a little wooden man and woman. They first form a house, but when the house catches fire they rearrange the blocks to form a fire engine. There is too much water, they reform the blocks into a boat. The blocks then become a truck and a train before again becoming a house. See also *Rosie's Walk*, not quite wordless but the second story happening in the background is totally wordless.

Do You Want to Be My Friend?, by Eric Carle (Puffin). A little mouse searching for a friend sees many animals but almost comes to grief before he finds a friend just his size.

Hug, by Jez Alborough (Walker). Not quite wordless – there are three words in the book. A tiny chimp has

lost his mother. He sees all the other baby animals being hugged and longs for a hug himself. With help from the elephant and other animals he is reunited with his mother and gets his longed-for hug.

Sunshine, by Jan Ormerod (Puffin, OP). A preschool child wakes and we follow her through the morning routine. She wakes her parents, then helps Dad prepare breakfast and take it back to bed. As her parents drift back to sleep she gets ready for kindergarten before waking them again. The illustrations catch the essence of early morning domestic activity with both movement and colour. Moonlight shows the same child as she goes through her evening routine.

The Hunter and the Animals, by Tomi de Paola (Holiday House, OP). This book, like others by this gifted illustrator, is very attractive. A hunter sets off to hunt in the woods but is unable to find any animals (although the reader can see them). When he goes to sleep the animals steal his gun and other supplies. He wakes to finds he is lost. The animals understand that he is sorry and guide him home.

The Snowman, by Raymond Briggs (Puffin). Many books show children's imaginary adventures but this is somewhat different. A small boy and the snowman he has built have magical fun. The illustrations are in soft colours that show the world blanketed in snow.

Watch Me, by Pamela Allen (Nelson, OP). This great little book is no longer in print, but check for it at your library. It shows a young rider on his tricycle who becomes more and more daring. He rides without using his feet then without using his hands, but when he attempts even more dangerous stunts he comes to grief. Other titles in this small square format are *Watch Me Now*, *Simon Said* and *Simon Did*.

Window, by Jeannie Baker (Random). This beautifully illustrated book has much to offer readers of all ages. It is a fine example of the collage work that Jeannie Baker does so well. Other wordless or near-wordless books by this artist are *Where the Forest Meets the Sea* and *Millicent*.

First Story Books

These are used to introduce babies and toddlers to stories. First story books are usually about the everyday routines of children and their families. Such things as meal-times, getting dressed, visits to and by relatives, shopping and playing are shown in these books. During their first two years children will meet different stories and begin to have favourites.

Often a small child or child-like animal is the central character. The sentences are usually short and often repeat key words or phrases. The text may rhyme or appeal through the sounds of the language. Some publishers use thicker card for the pages of these books so that they will withstand rough handling.

- The everyday events that are the subject of these
  books give preschoolers a sense of security, learning
  that others feel and behave as they do. They find that
  other children may be afraid of the dark, do not want
  to use a potty, find playgroup scary or have problems
  with the arrival of a new baby.

- Through these stories children learn the
  'conventions of stories'. They learn that a story has
  a beginning, a middle and an end. When the ending
  is satisfying children can see 'Yes, that's how it is.'

- As stories are read to them children observe how
  books work (the conventions of print). They
  understand that there is a 'right way up' for books
  and that adults read from the front to the back. They
  may realise that adults look at the cover to find the
  name of the book. As the adult reads to them they
  begin to see that stories are associated with the
  marks on the page. They begin to have favourite
  books and stories and realise that each time an adult
  shares *that* particular book they will hear *that* story.

- Children begin to predict what will happen next in
  the story. This is a valuable skill for when they begin
  formal instruction in reading. Being able to predict

helps the new reader to anticipate what is to come
and so make sense of the text.

- The child's vocabulary is expanded and enriched.
  In *Lulu* by Dorothy Butler the story tells how other
  cats were afraid but 'Lulu was calm and courageous'.
  In *Hairy Maclary's Rumpus at the Vet* by Linley Dodd we
  meet 'miserable dogs, cantankerous cats ...'.

- These books help preschoolers learn that reading
  brings fun and enjoyment. This is important in
  developing a positive attitude to books and reading.

- Through stories preschoolers' listening skills are
  helped. Listening is very important since much of
  what we learn comes through listening. Many young
  children have learnt to 'turn off' to sounds around
  them. Sharing enjoyable, entertaining stories is a fun
  way to help develop listening skills.

BOOKS TO LOOK FOR

Remember, some of these titles may be out of print but
look for them in your local library.

Brand New Baby, by Bob Graham (Walker). This brings
together four little stories that were first available as
separate books. They are *Waiting for the New Baby*,
Visiting the New Baby, *Bringing Home the New Baby* and

Getting to Know the New Baby. The Arnold family, with preschoolers Edward and Wendy, are trying to get used to the changes that a new baby brings. Eventually baby Walter settles in and family life goes on happily.

Dreadful David, by Sally Farrell Odgers (Omnibus). David's Mum takes him to stay with his Gran. On the way he scatters the contents of his mother's handbag along the road and at Gran's he gets up to all sorts of mischief. But he had not reckoned on his Gran's approach to bad behaviour.

Giving, by Shirley Hughes (Walker). The little girl in this appealing book is about three and she explores the idea of giving within her family: giving a kiss, a present, a smile, a ride on Dad's shoulders, and Dad giving comfort and a band-aid when she is given a scratch from the cat. Three other titles in the series are *Chatting*, *Hiding* and *Bouncing*.

Gran and Grandpa, by Helen Oxenbury (Walker). This shows a young girl visiting her grandparents and the fun she has even though it may wear out the oldies. Others in the series are *The Check-up*, *The Dancing Class*, *Playschool* and *Our Dog*.

Happy Birthday Sam, by Pat Hutchins (Puffin). Sam is having another birthday and is disappointed to find he is still too short to reach the door handle. But his grandfather's gift solves his problem. Other books by Pat Hutchins that show the problems of being the smallest in the family are *Titch*, *You'll Soon Grow Into Them Titch* and *Tidy Titch*.

Has Anyone Here Seen William?, by Bob Graham (Viking Kestrel). William is the youngest and is often over-looked by the family until someone realises he is missing. This happens at home, on picnics and even at the shops. When William is found he is usually in the middle of something – an overturned bookcase, a duck pond or a shop window display! But when he is missing at his birthday party he is not far away.

I Want My Potty, by Tony Ross (Collins). The little princess discovers there is something better than nappies but she cannot always find her potty when she needs it. Children who no longer need a potty seem to find this really funny. See also *On Your Potty*.

I'm Not Sleepy, by Colin & Jacquie Hawkins (Walker). Baby bear does not want to go to sleep and thinks up all sorts of excuses. But finally, after a cuddle from Mum, he snoozes off.

Just Like Me, by Jan Ormerod (Walker). A preschooler has been told by her grandma that her baby brother is just like her. She finds this difficult to believe because he does such strange things, but she thinks that when he is older he may be 'just like me'. Other titles in the series are *Our Ollie* and *Silly Goose*.

Little Pink Pig, by Pat Hutchins (Julia MacRae). As it is bedtime mother pig tries to hurry little pink pig home. But everything in the farmyard seems to delay this little pink pig.

Messy Baby, by Jan Ormerod (Walker). This delightful little book depicts a young dad showing baby, who is at the crawling stage, how to put away toys and such.

What Dad doesn't realise is that baby is following him undoing all his work. This title is one in the series Dad and Me. Other titles are *Dad's Back*, *Reading* and *Sleeping*.

Mum's Home, by Jan Ormerod (Walker). These little books are similar in format to the Dad and Me series but this collection features Mum and Me. We see Mum and baby sharing their day's activities at home. Titles include *Bend and Stretch*, *Making Friends* and *This Little Nose*.

My Best Friend, by Pat Hutchins (Julia MacRae). When her friend comes to stay the heroine of this tale finds that her friend can run faster, climb higher and jump further than she can. She can even eat spaghetti without dropping any on the table! But when the light is out and the wind blows the curtains around, the best friend needs reassurance from the heroine that there is no monster in the room.

My Brown Bear Barney, by Dorothy Butler, illustrated by Elizabeth Fuller (Angus & Robertson). This is told by a preschooler. She takes her brown bear Barney everywhere, but when she begins school she says

Barney will have to stay home. By the same author, *My Brown Bear Barney in Trouble*.

Noisy Nora, by Rosemary Wells (Collins). Nora is always making a noise but no one notices her. She decides to run away and only when things are quiet is she missed. Nora is a small mouse, but children can sympathise with the feeling of being overlooked in a busy home.

On Your Potty, by Virginia Miller (Walker). Bartholomew is told to use the potty but cannot. Later when he is playing he needs to find the potty quickly! Bartholomew and his dad George are bears, but toddlers will sympathise with Bartholomew and parents will relate to George. Other titles about them are *Eat Your Dinner* and *Get Into Bed!*

Peter's Chair, by Ezra Jack Keats (Red Fox). Peter's baby sister has arrived and all his baby things are being repainted. He decides that his little blue chair will not become pink like everything else. He packs up and leaves (as far as the footpath outside his home). But when he realises the chair is now too small for him he reconsiders his position as a big brother and helps Dad paint it.

Sleep Time, by Libby Gleeson (Ashton Scholastic). A little girl is put to bed to sleep. But she objects as it is not dark. She tries unsuccessfully to find someone else to have her sleep for her. Compare this with *Can't You Sleep Little Bear?*, *Get Into Bed!* and *I'm Not Sleepy*.

The Red Woollen Blanket, by Bob Graham (Puffin). This is a great book that starts with Julia being given a red woollen blanket when she is born. She and her blanket cannot be separated in her first five years and by the time she begins school there is not much of her blanket left. Another book on this theme is *Geraldine's Blanket* by Holly Keller.

Tom and Pippo's Day, by Helen Oxenbury (Walker). Tom and his toy monkey Pippo feature in a number of books by this outstanding illustrator.

Flap and Other
Manipulative Books

This type of book allows infants to see that reading is fun. But although there are many such books available, not all reach the high standard we should expect in books for children.

THEIR VALUE FOR CHILDREN

- The first value is that of enjoyment. Toddlers delight in reading these over and over again. Most families find that their copies become worn out not from misuse but from overuse. Parents who share these with their infants are reinforcing the idea that books are enjoyable. If children are to succeed with reading as they grow older it is essential that their early experiences with books are fun.

- Manipulating the flaps on these books will help
  develop the child's hand–eye co-ordination. Children
  need to be able to focus on an area, bring their hands
  and fingers to that position and then use their hands.
  Good hand–eye co-ordination is needed if children
  are to learn to feed themselves, dress, draw, build
  with blocks, follow words across a page of print or
  learn to write.

- These simple, enjoyable little books encourage
  children to predict what will be under the flap.
  Prediction is a very valuable skill for making sense
  of what is read. This was not always recognised in
  the past, when children were reprimanded for
  'guessing'. But it is an essential skill if readers are
  to make sense of what they read.

HOW TO SELECT BOOKS

When selecting flap books to use with preschool children
consider both the content and the structure.

Content

- Check the subject of the book. It should be within
  the interest range of the child who will use it. Spot
  books and Buster books have succeeded because Spot's
  and Buster's interests are those of preschool children.

- Look at the amount of detail in the illustrations. If a page is very 'busy' with many small, detailed illustrations the book is better suited to older children.

Structure

- Better quality flap books have pages made of card rather than the paper of picture books. This allows them to withstand constant use.
- Look at the size of the flap that is to be turned. Some books have tiny flaps. These may be suitable for school-aged children but they are too fiddly for toddlers, who are likely to tear them off the page. Others have very large flaps, which can also be a problem for small fingers to turn and replace.
- Check the amount of text and where it is placed on the page. Spot books have very little text and it is placed well away from the illustrations. Some books have far too much writing for preschool children. If most of the text is in speech balloons the books are for older readers who will enjoy them.
- Check the size of the print. Print that is large and clear will help when children begin to read independently.
- For preschool children, the overall size of the book

should be considered. Some large books are just too difficult for them to hold, turn pages and manipulate flaps.

• Some books use metal split pins to secure wheel-like flaps that turn. Always check that these cannot fall out – children may put them in their mouth or cut themselves.

While considering flap books it would be timely to look at books that have peepholes in the pages. Many of these, such as Carol Jones' *This Old Man*, allow the child to predict what will come next.

However, some peephole books give a view of the world that may be impossible for toddlers to comprehend. Young children, according to the psychologist Piaget, can only see the world from their perspective. Yet some of these books show a child looking at an object from the outside and then show a view from the inside of the same object, such as outside and inside a letterbox – this is a bit too much of an imaginative leap for very young children.

FLAP BOOKS TO LOOK FOR

Baby Goz, by Steve Weatherill (Koala Books). This is similar to *Are You My Mother?* by Eastman. A baby gosling hatches from a large egg and goes in search of his mother. The flap on each page is the egg shape from which Goz hatched. But now it conceals in turn a frog, a cat and a dog before Goz finds his mother and is hustled off for a swimming lesson. Another Goz book that is enjoyed by two- to three-year-olds is *When I Grow Up*, which shows how growing things change – a tadpole becomes a frog, a grub a butterfly, and an acorn grows to an oak tree.

Buster's Day, by Rod Campbell (Macmillan). From early morning until bedtime Buster explores inside and outside his home. The reader is encouraged to guess what Buster will find in cupboards, under a leaf or behind the bedroom curtain. Other titles are *Buster Gets Dressed* and *Buster Goes to Playgroup*.

Dear Zoo, by Eric Hill (Puffin). In this book, by the creator of the Spot books, a young child tells how he wants a pet. The zoo sends different animals but none is right. Each animal is hidden under a flap. It is not until the last animal arrives that the boy finds a pet that is just right.

Mog and Barnaby, by Judith Kerr (Collins). Mog the cat is known to toddlers through Mog board books and Mog story books. In this book Mog and his human family are visited by a very active little dog called Barnaby. Poor Mog has a dreadful time as Barnaby playfully jumps all over him.

My Presents, by Rod Campbell (Picturemac). Someone has had a birthday and this book shows the presents. On each page the child is invited to guess what is inside the brightly wrapped gifts and then to lift the wrapping and see.

Noisy Farm, by Rod Campbell (Lothian). In this the reader is invited to go on a walk around the farm, lift the flaps and discover which animals are making noises.

Oh Dear!, by Rod Campbell (Picturemac). Buster is at

Grandma's farm and sets off to find eggs. As he goes around the farmyard he looks in many places before he finds the right place for new eggs.

Spot's First Walk, by Eric Hill (Puffin). Spot is the small yellow pup who lives with Sally and Sam. In this book Spot explores the surroundings of his own yard and the world through the fence. Other Spot books are *Where's Spot?*, *Spot's Birthday Party*, *Spot's First Christmas*, *Spot's Baby Sister*, *Spot Goes to the Park*, *Spot Stays Overnight* and *Spot Goes to School*.

Surprise, by Kerry Argent (Omnibus). Wombat's birthday surprise is being prepared by his friends. Wombat is impatient and searches the house but does not uncover his gift until everything is ready for a party.

PEEPHOLE BOOKS TO LOOK FOR

Hickory Dickory Dock, illustrated by Carol Jones (Angus & Robertson). This has a number of nursery rhymes such as 'Little Bo-peep', 'Hey diddle diddle' and 'Hickory dickory dock'. Like *This Old Man* there are circles cut into the pages to allow a peep at what is to come.

Old Macdonald had a Farm, illustrated by Carol Jones (Angus & Robertson). This is the song that most families know. The reader can see through the peepholes to find which animal will be introduced next on Macdonald's farm.

Peepo, by Allan & Janet Ahlberg (Puffin). This shows an English family at home. The holes in the pages gives a glimpse of what will be discovered when the page is turned.

This Old Man, illustrated by Carol Jones (Angus & Robertson). This shows the song that most youngsters learn before school. The only characters are a little girl and the old man. The book is arranged with circular holes in alternate pages. Through these holes the reader can see enough of the next page to continue the song before the page is turned. The full-page illustrations are crammed with detail that will reward careful examination. There are many opportunities to discuss the illustrations as the old man and the child move around their country home during different seasons.

Early Concept Books

Twenty-five years ago, teachers did not expect children beginning school to understand the concepts listed below, as many of them were taught in the first year of school. Children are now expected to have been introduced to these concepts before they begin formal schooling.

THEIR VALUE FOR TODDLERS

These books will help children learn some vital concepts.

- Colour: knowing the names of colours.
- Shapes: recognising squares, triangles, circles and rectangles.
- Size: differentiating between 'big' and 'little'.
- Position: understanding concepts of place – by, between, under, over, in, out, through.

- Time: understanding different times of the day, such as breakfast-time, lunch-time and bed-time.
- Number: understanding simple number groups, such as 1, 2, 3 for things around them.

These concepts and others such as days of the week and months of the year can be introduced through good picture books.

Books to look for

Colour

Brown Bear, Brown Bear, What Do You See?, by Bill Martin, illustrated by Eric Carle (Collins). This delightful book uses repetition to introduce a range of animals all of different colours.

Kippers Book of Colours, by Mick Inkpen (Hodder). Kipper the pup helps young readers discover colours. Red is a bowl of strawberries, orange is a drink sipped through a very twisty straw and purple is a purple monster. These are presented against a white background that makes the colours stand out clearly.

Moo, Moo Brown Cow Have You Any . . ., by Jakki Wood, illustrated by Roger Bonner (Collins). This book begins much like 'Baa, baa black sheep', but each time

the little cat greets an animal we not only learn its
colour but the name of its baby (calf, lambs, kids,
goslings). The number of young animals grows from
one calf to ten small trout fry.

My Little Book of Colours, by Jan Ormerod (Walker).
This small square book is a delight. It begins with
a line of clean clothes, each item a different colour.
A small child begins to dress and on each page he puts
on clothing of a different colour: white underwear,
green T-shirt, red jumper, blue overalls and black
boots. Because of the child playing in brown dirt we
then meet an orange towel and yellow pyjamas.

Paddington's Colours, by Michael Bond (Collins). This
large hard-covered book has only a few words on
each page. The illustrations make it certain that young
readers will enjoy having Paddington teach them
about colours.

The Bad Babies Book of Colours, by Tony Bradman (Red
Fox). The bad babies are all invited to William's birthday party. They share food, games and fun and along
the way learn about the colours in their world.

Shapes

Fuzzy Yellow Ducklings, by Matthew Van Fleet (Dial).

This sturdy book introduces circle, triangle, square, oval and line shapes through interesting textures. Under each flap is a surprise. See also *Spotted Yellow Frogs*, which introduces solid shapes such as a cube, cone and cylinder.

What's Round, by Dick Bruna (ABC Books). The reader begins with a clock face then meets other things that are round, from cherries to wheels. Dick Bruna's clear illustrations are a sound introduction to shapes.

Opposites

Bathwater's Hot, by Shirley Hughes (Hodder). A family shows things that are opposites, beginning with bathwater that is hot and seawater that is cold. A lovely way to introduce these concepts in a story of family fun.

Good Days, Bad Days, by Catherine & Laurence Anholt (Orchard). This has wonderful illustrations that show opposites such as bad days and good days.

Kipper's Book of Opposites, by Mick Inkpen (Hodder). This small square book presents a set of opposites on each double-page spread. Kipper the playful little dog shows such opposites as big/small, night/day, long/short, slow/fast, up/down, happy/sad and in/out.

Nice and Nasty: A Book of Opposites, by Nick Butter-
worth & Mick Inkpen (Hodder). This shows contrasting words in a fun way. Rough and smooth are
depicted by a smooth frog and a rough-skinned toad;
weak and strong is a mouse trying to push an elephant.

Opposites, by Gwenda Turner (Puffin). Through very
life-like illustrations we meet such opposites as wet
and dry, on and off, long and short.

Paddington's Opposites, by Michael Bond (Collins).
Paddington is known to many young readers. In this
large colourful book with not much text, Paddington
helps preschoolers to learn about opposites.

Simpkin, by Quentin Blake (Jonathan Cape). Like
many of Quentin Blake's characters, Simpkin lives in
a dreadful muddle, going from one extreme to the
other. This is an unusual way to show opposites and is
really fun.

Days of the week

Cookie's Week, by Cindy Ward, illustrated by Tomi de
Paola (Scholastic). Starting on Monday, when he falls
in the toilet, Cookie the cat goes through the week
causing uproar in the house.

Mr Wolf's Week, by Colin & Jacqui Hawkins (Collins

Young Lions). This is a humorous way of looking at the days of the week. Mr Wolf has problems as each day has a different set of weather conditions that he must face.

My Brown Bear Barney in Trouble, by Dorothy Butler. This story is told by a preschooler who takes Barney everywhere.

Oliver's Vegetables, by Vivian French, illustrated by Alison Bartlett (Hodder). Oliver eats no vegetables except potato chips. But at Grandpa's he can only have chips if he can find where the potatoes grow. He agrees to eat any vegetable that he pulls up during his search for the potatoes. Each day he samples, and likes, a different vegetable. It is Sunday before he finds the potatoes.

Pig Out, by Sascha Hutchinson (Lothian). Pigs enjoy different foods on each day of the week. Each food begins with the letter 'P'. Small readers approve of Sunday's food – pizza. The illustrations are in paper collage.

The Very Hungry Caterpillar, by Eric Carle (Puffin). A small green grub eats its way through the week in this outstanding picture book that introduces numbers, days of the week and the butterfly's lifecycle.

What a Week!, by Robyn Ryan, illustrated by Craig Smith (Playworks Resource Unit, Prahran, Victoria). Each day Sam is involved in something different: at the pool, the supermarket, or playgroup. Only through the illustrations do we learn that Sam has a disability and needs a walking frame.

Months of the year

A House for Hermit Crab, by Eric Carle (Hamish Hamilton). Hermit Crab begins to search for a new home in January. In February he finds the right one but it needs decorating. During the following months we see the changes to his home and the friends he makes. *The Bad Babies Book of Months*, by Tony Bradman (Red Fox). The bad babies are a group of preschoolers who certainly deserve the title 'Bad Babies'. They are naughty every month of the year.

The Gumnuts' Year, illustrated by Vicky Kitanov (Collins). This is a beautifully illustrated book depicting the seasons in Australia and showing Australian flora and fauna. Adults are given additional information on the animals, birds, insects and plants that are shown.

Position or place

Henry's Ball, by Rod Campbell (Campbell Books). Henry looks everywhere for his ball. The reader meets the concepts of into, along, under, between and through.

Rosie's Walk, by Pat Hutchins (Random Century). Rosie the hen goes for a walk, followed by a sly fox. In following Rosie, the reader sees her go across, around, over, under, through and past various parts of the farm.

Time

Dog In Cat Out, by Gillian Rubinstein, illustrated by Ann James (Omnibus). This has very little text (only four different words!) and shows the activities of a household over a day. A clock on the left-hand page shows the time from early morning until night.

What's the Time Mr Wolf?, by Colin & Jacqui Hawkins
(Collins). Mr Wolf has to know the time to do everything during one day. The illustrations are large and
appeal to preschoolers.

Picture Books

When parents or grandparents visit bookshops or libraries they are confronted with a great range of books from which to choose. Some of these are outstanding and others are mundane. Some will become classics that children will continue to enjoy for years; others will be forgotten within a few months.

THEIR VALUE FOR CHILDREN

Picture books are usually more complex than first story books, and entertain both the child and the adult. At the same time these books can give infants and preschoolers an interest in new words. Children who have heard Pamela Allen's *Bertie and the Bear* learn that many sounds together can make an 'incredible' noise. Three-year-olds with whom I've shared the story love to experiment with this new word.

Most young children first meet kangaroos, possums, wombats and the more exotic animals through picture books. Children in Australia may see snowy fields and frozen ponds only in books. These experiences are absorbed and the new words added to their growing vocabulary.

In addition, picture books help develop the skills and knowledge that are needed in learning to read. As children share picture books they become aware of how books work – the conventions of print. They learn that our books read from front to back, from top to bottom and from left to right. These concepts are learned while sharing books with an experienced reader, either an older sibling or an adult.

In homes where reading is a normal activity and shared with even the youngest members, children have little or no fear of learning to read. It is seen as something that will happen as a matter of course because everyone at home does it! It is not unusual in such homes to find a pre-school child 'reading' a favourite book. They have the book open and as they tell the story (because they know it very well) they turn the page and may even point to the print on the page.

Familiarity with stories and books leads to young children becoming aware of the difference between 'book language' and spoken language. They understand that 'once upon a time' will begin a story that may be about bears, princesses or fairy godmothers.

BOOKS TO LOOK FOR

A Proper Little Lady, by Nette Hilton, illustrated by Cathy Wilcox (Collins). When Annabella Jones dresses to go out she looks a 'proper little lady' with her flouncy dress, jingling chains, flowered hat, lacy gloves and smart shoes. But after she climbs a tree, plays football and rides a billycart she returns looking a very bedraggled 'little lady'. A great use of language supported by humorous illustration.

Alexander's Outing, by Pamela Allen (Puffin). Mother Duck is taking her brood of ducklings for a walk. Although his brothers and sisters stay close behind their mother and watch where they are going, Alexander does not! As a result he falls into a deep hole and the people nearby have to find a means of rescuing him.

Alfie Gives a Hand, by Shirley Hughes (Random

House). When Alfie is invited to a birthday party he is too shy to go without his special blanket. Bernard, the birthday boy, is making life difficult for another guest who is also very shy so Alfie puts aside his blanket to hold her hand. Other stories about Alfie are *Alfie Gets in First*, *One Evening at Alfie's* and *Alfie's Feet*. Shirley Hughes' family stories are spot-on.

Arthur, by Amanda Graham, illustrated by Donna Gynell (Era). Children love Arthur, the story of a funny brown dog in a petshop window. He tries to be like the more popular animals in an effort to find a home, but despite his efforts he is not sold. Then Melanie and her grandfather arrive. Other stories about Arthur are *Educating Arthur* and *Always Arthur*.

Belinda, by Pamela Allen (Puffin). This story appeals to preschoolers and older children. When Old Tom is left home to look after the farm he has trouble milking Belinda, who is always milked by Bessie. But he hits on a novel way of overcoming the problem.

Bertie and the Bear, by Pamela Allen (Puffin). This is fun and offers the chance to make lots of noise. The story tells how the whole court becomes involved in chasing after the bear and Bertie.

Can't You Sleep Little Bear?, by Martin Waddell, illustrated by Barbara Firth (Walker). Little Bear has been tucked up in bed and Big Bear has settled down to read. But Little Bear has problems settling down. The illustrations are a delight. This story of Little Bear could be the story of any little person who finds excuses for not staying in bed. The same two bears appear in *Time to Go Home Little Bear*, *You and Me Little Bear* and *Well Done! Little Bear*.

Celeste Sails to Spain, by Alison Lester (Hodder). A group of seven children are shown with their individual likes, dislikes and interests. Other titles in the same format are *Clive Eats Alligators*, *Rosie Sips Spiders*, *Tessa Snaps Snakes*, *When Frank was Four* and *Ernie Dances to the Didgeridoo*.

Clippity-Clop, by Pamela Allen (Puffin). This is the story of how a little old woman and little old man have loaded their two obstinate donkeys and try to get them to move. Each tries a different way. Like other books by this award-winning author, the sound effects are wonderful.

Crusher is Coming, by Bob Graham (Lothian). Like all Bob Graham's books, this is a domestic drama. Peter has invited his football-playing friend to visit after school and, afraid that Crusher will think him a sissy, has offloaded all his soft toys on to his baby sister Claire. But Crusher's interests are a surprise to Peter.

Greetings from Sandy Beach, by Bob Graham (Lothian). A weekend trip to the beach looks as if it might become a nightmare. The family arrive at the same time as a motorcycle gang and a busload of children on a camping excursion. But appearances can be deceiving.

Hairy Maclary from Donaldson's Dairy, by Linley Dodd (Puffin). This is a great story that children love to hear. Hairy Maclary is a small black dog and with his other doggy friends goes off to explore the town. But when they meet Scarface Claw, 'The toughest Tom in town', they all hurry back home to safety. Other titles to look for are *Hairy Maclary's Bone*, *Hairy Maclary's Rumpus at the Vet*, *Hairy Maclary's Caterwaul Caper* and *Hairy Maclary Scattercat*.

Hattie and the Fox, by Mem Fox, illustrated by Patricia Mullins (Ashton Scholastic). Hattie is a large black hen who is trying to warn the other farm animals about an intruder that only she can see. This is beautifully illustrated in torn tissue collage.

I Wish I Had a Pirate Suit, by Pamela Allen (Puffin). This shows the problems of being the younger child and always having to play games devised by the older child. Great illustrations show the imagination of children at play.

I'm Green and I'm Grumpy, by Alison Lester (Puffin). This is a great little book about dressing up. Half-pages are used to hide the next character dressed in fancy costume. By completing the rhyme, readers can guess what the child will be dressed up as next. A companion book is *Monsters are Knocking*.

Koala Lou, by Mem Fox (Puffin). Because she longs for her mother to tell her that she loves her, Koala Lou is desperate to win the tree-climbing event at the

Bush Olympics. It is only when she is beaten that she learns that her mother has always loved her.

Mr Magnolia, by Quentin Blake (Random Century). This is fun to read aloud because of the rhymes and rhythm. Mr Magnolia is a very strange character whose life is filled with odd things but he has one real problem – he has only one boot!

Mr McGee and the Biting Flea, by Pamela Allen (Puffin). Mr McGee is having fun at the beach until a flea from a passing dog begins to bite him. The illustrations of Mr McGee taking off his clothes to rid himself of the flea are fun.

Possum Magic, by Mem Fox, illustrated by Julie Vivas (Omnibus). Children love this beautifully illustrated book. Grandma Poss has made Hush invisible to keep her safe but cannot remember how to undo the spell. They journey around Australia in an effort to solve the problem.

Rosie's Walk, by Pat Hutchins (Puffin). Rosie the hen goes for a walk, followed by a sly fox. In following Rosie, the reader sees her go across, around, over, under, through and past various parts of the farm.

The Very Hungry Caterpillar, by Eric Carle. A small green grub eats its way through the week in this outstanding picture book that introduces numbers, days of the week and the butterfly's lifecycle.

The Very Worst Monster, by Pat Hutchins (Bodley Head). When Billy Monster is born everyone makes a fuss of him and ignores his sister, Hazel. They are sure he will be the worst monster in the world. Hazel declares she is, but no one hears her. However, Hazel proves she is by giving the baby away! Others in the series are *Where's the Baby?*, *Silly Billy*, *Three Star Billy* and *It's My Birthday*.

We're Going on a Bear Hunt, by Michael Rosen, illustrated by Helen Oxenbury (Walker). This is great for reading aloud as it has lots of repetition. Helen Oxenbury's illustrations show Dad and the kids in soft muted colours.

Where the Wild Things Are, by Maurice Sendak (Puffin). When Max is sent to his room for being naughty he sails off to the land where the wild things are. He becomes king of all the wild things but when he gets lonely he comes home to 'where someone loves him best of all'.

Who Sank the Boat?, by Pamela Allen (Puffin). As the animals begin to pile into the small rowboat it looks very unsteady. But it does not sink with the cow, the donkey or the sheep. Who did sink the boat?

Culturally Inclusive

Picture Books

'Culturally inclusive literature' means books that show people from diverse cultures. These may include books that show our multicultural society, books set in countries other than Australia or folktales from any country.

THEIR VALUE TO CHILDREN

- Many of us have ties to cultures that began in Europe, Asia, Africa, America, the Pacific islands or Australia before white occupation. Picture books can present people from these different cultures in a way that children can understand.
- Stories which show that children are much the same everywhere can help develop tolerance.
- Books about children who are not from white

Anglo-Saxon families can help raise the self-esteem of children with similar backgrounds.

Books depicting a multicultural society

Children's books show that people from many cultural backgrounds are all part of our society. However, when choosing such books look at the characters from different ethnic backgrounds. Do they have a real place in the story or have they been included merely to make the story 'politically correct'? The following picture books have characters from a variety of cultures. Not all are set in Australia but they show that different cultures make up modern society.

A Balloon for Grandad, by Nigel Gray, illustrated by Jane Ray (Orchard). When Sam's red balloon floats

away his dad suggests that the balloon has gone to visit Grandad Abdulla. Sam imagines its journey across the sea, over the desert, then over a river to an island where his grandfather lives tending his goats and dates.

A Nice Walk in the Jungle, by Nan Bodsworth (Viking). This shows a class of children from different ethnic backgrounds. The school is somewhere in the northern part of Australia and the mixture in the class reflects what is common in many classrooms today.

Big Dog, by Libby Gleeson, illustrated by Armin Greder (Ashton Scholastic). This book shows a group of children trying to help the youngest, who is afraid of a dog that lives nearby. To do this they use a Chinese dragon figure owned by one of the families. But the dog turns out to be friendly and the problem is resolved.

Cleversticks, by Bernard Ashley, illustrated by Derek Brazell (Collins). This book may be used for many age groups. Ling Sung is a kindergarten child who feels inadequate because he does not have the skills that other children have. But when he demonstrates how to use chopsticks he finds out he has a skill that no one else does. He helps the others with chopsticks and

they show him how to put on his coat, write his name
and tie his art smock.

Going for Oysters, by Jeanie Adams (Omnibus). At
Aurukun there is a wonderful family gathering and
everyone sets off to the river to gather oysters. But
the children forget grandfather's warning.

Going Home, by Margaret Wild, illustrated by Wayne
Harris (Ashton Scholastic). This book is set in a hospital ward where Hugo (whose family is Eurasian),
Nirimala (who is Indian) and Simon (who is Caucasian)
discover something magic.

I Won't Go There Again, by Susan Hill, illustrated by Jim
Bispham (Julia MacRae). Like Cleversticks, this book
is set in a kindergarten. The children are a general
cross-section of those who would be found in most
kindergartens in large cities today. This is a good
story about understanding.

Mr Plunkett's Pool, by Gillian Rubinstein, illustrated by
Terry Denton (Random Century). Mr Plunkett buys
and modernises an old mansion. When he installs
a pool the local children want to swim with him. The
children are from a variety of ethnic backgrounds.

Mum Goes to Work, by Libby Gleeson, illustrated by Penny Azar (Ashton Scholastic). This book shows an inner-city childcare centre with parents from many different ethnic backgrounds dropping off their children and meeting each other. The day's events are shown through the activities of mothers and children.

My Best Friend, by Pat Hutchins. The two friends in this story are small West Indian girls. But the fun they share is that of small friends anywhere. When her friend comes to stay, the heroine of this tale finds that her friend can run faster, climb higher and jump further than she can. She can even eat spaghetti without dropping any on the table! But when the light is out and the wind blows the curtains around, the best friend needs reassurance from the heroine that there is no monster in the room.

Pigs and Honey, by Jeanie Adams (Omnibus). This is the story of a contemporary Aboriginal family living at Aurukun on Cape York Peninsula. The family go bush to hunt wild pigs and gather honey.

The Kinder Hat, by Morag Loh, illustrated by Donna Rawlins (Hyland House). A kindergarten girl has a special surprise for her mum – a hat made from an

ice-cream container. Mum proudly wears her gift all
the way home. The kindergarten has students from
different ethnic groups. This is shown through the
children's names displayed with their work, notices
in several languages and the appearance of the children themselves.

Tucker's Mob, by Christabel Mattingley, illustrated by
Jeanie Adams (Omnibus). Tucker the cat follows the
children Sunny, Sam and Sue to school at the Barunga
Aboriginal Community. Sam's picture of Tucker is
the start of a special book.

**Books with settings that can extend children's view
of the world**

Ayu and the Perfect Moon, by David Cox (Macmillan
Connections Pack). A Balinese grandmother tells her
granddaughter about her childhood when she danced
in a special festival on the night of the full moon.

Handa's Surprise, by Eileen Brown (Walker). An African girl is taking a basket of fruit as a gift to her friend. As she walks along with the basket on her head, every piece is stolen by a different wild animal. But an angry goat causes her basket to be refilled with tangerines.

Is it True Grandfather?, by Wendy Lohse, illustrated by Jenny Sands (Scholastic). This beautiful book is set in the Seychelles and shows that children don't change much from one generation to the next – they have the same sense of adventure and the same fears.

Miss Bunkle's Umbrella, by David Cox (Macmillian Connections Pack). This tells of an older tourist who becomes separated from her tourist group in Java and learns so much from the local people, who entertain her.

The Boss, by Allan Baillie, illustrated by Fiona O'Beirne (Scholastic). The Boss is a small Chinese boy who rules his family from morning to night.

Folktales from other cultures

Folktales occur in all cultures. The following are some that are available in picture book format.

Mufaro's Beautiful Daughters, by John Steptoe (Hodder & Stoughton). This beautifully illustrated story tells how the king decided which of the beautiful daughters of Mufaro should become his queen.

The Great Big Enormous Turnip, by Alexei Tolstoy, illustrated by Helen Oxenbury (Picture Mammoth). This well-known story from Russia tells how the smallest can help those who are stronger.

The Mouse Bride, by Joy Cowley, illustrated by David Christiana (Ashton Scholastic). This is a beautifully illustrated version of a folktale that is told in Africa, Central America and many Asian countries. A small mouse sets off to find the strongest husband in the world. Her search takes her full circle, back to home.

The Old Woman and the Red Pumpkin, by Betsy Bang, illustrated by Rachel Merriman (Walker). When an old woman sets off to visit her granddaughter she meets a jackal, a tiger and a bear. Each want to eat her. But she convinces them that she is too skinny and if they wait for her to return she will be much fatter. On her return journey she has a way to outwit the animals.

The Two Bullies, by Junko Morimoto (Red Fox). This story explains why a statue called Ni-ou stands guard outside the temple of Hachiman in Japan. Ni-ou was the strongest man in Japan. When he hears about a strong man in China called Dokkoi he sets out to fight him. But when Ni-ou sees how strong Dokkoi is and realises Dokkoi may beat him, he flees. Only a gift given by the god Hachiman, disguised as a priest, saves Ni-ou from defeat.

Tikki Tikki Tembo, by Arlene Mosel, illustrated by Blair Lent (Owlet, Henry Holt &Co.). This is an old book but look for it in your library as it reads aloud really well. It explains why Chinese children have such short names. When a boy had a really long name, such as Tikki Tikki Tembo No Sa Rembo Chari Bari Ruchi Pip Piri Pembo, it was difficult to call for help when he fell into the well.

Preparation for
Early Reading

Children who live in homes where reading is valued, where they have been surrounded by books, handled books, visited libraries and enjoyed listening to stories have a great advantage when they begin school. They have already gained many of the skills for learning to read. And they have learnt these skills while having fun. These children see reading as something that is a normal activity to be enjoyed, not a difficult 'school-only' activity. They assume that they will learn to read because every one at home does.

HOW TO SELECT BOOKS

Sharing any books that are enjoyable will help in developing early reading skills, but there are some books that will give children an even greater advantage. In choosing books to use with preschoolers, look for those that have one or more of the following:

- repetition
- rhyme
- an established pattern so that your child can see what comes next
- illustrations that help the child to tell the story.

After several readings of *Brown Bear, Brown Bear, What Do You See?* children from three years of age are able to join in and 'read'. They can use the pattern of this story, with its question, answers and picture clues, to retell the story. Educators call this 'reading behaviour', which means children are using the book the way they have seen adults use it. Such children begin school greatly advantaged.

BOOKS TO LOOK FOR

Books with repetition

> *Boo to a Goose*, by Mem Fox, illustrated by David Martin (Hodder Children's Books). Children can join in and 'read' this from the second or third page. On a second reading they can use the illustrations to fill in the parts that are not repeated.

> *Brown Bear, Brown Bear, What Do You See?*, by Bill Martin

(Picture Lions). This delightful book uses repetition to introduce a range of animals all of different colours.

Drummer Hoff, by Barbara Emberley, illustrated by Ed Emberly (Bodley Head). In this book with unusual illustrations a procession of military personnel bring the different parts needed to construct a cannon. It is Drummer Hoff who fires it. Repetition and rhyme encourages children to join in 'reading'.

Hairy Maclary from Donaldson's Dairy, by Linley Dodd (Puffin). Hairy Maclary and his doggy friends have become a favourite with children across Australia. My copy is almost worn out with frequent readings. But even a child hearing it for the first time is able to join in with the adult reader and 'read' because the pattern is predictable.

Hattie and the Fox, by Mem Fox, illustrated by Patricia Mullins (Ashton Scholastic). Hattie is a large black hen who is trying to warn the other farm animals about an intruder that only she can see. This is beautifully illustrated in torn tissue collage.

'I Don't Care!' Said the Bear, by Colin West (Walker). Three- and four-year-olds soon recognise the pattern

in this story about a big brown bear who didn't care when he was followed by a goose, a moose, a snake or even a wolf. But he ran off home when he saw a tiny mouse.

I Went Walking, by Sue Machin, illustrated by Julie Vivas (Omnibus). Every second opening repeats the words 'I went walking. What did you see?' A clue to the answer is given in the illustration. Children recognise the pattern and can 'read' it after having heard it once or twice.

Mr Magnolia, by Quentin Blake (Random Century). This is fun to read aloud because of the rhymes and rhythm. Mr Magnolia is a very strange character whose life is filled with odd things but he has one real problem – he has only one boot!

Nicketty-Nacketty, Noo-Noo-Noo, by Joy Cowley, illustrated by Tracey Moroney (Scholastic). A wee woman is walking through the woods when she is kidnapped by an ogre called Gobbler Magoo. He wants her to make him a nice tasty stew. And she does... from glue. Great fun.

Time for Bed, by Mem Fox, illustrated by Jane Dyer (Omnibus). This gentle story about animals and their mothers has much repetition. The illustrations are appealing and children soon want to read it for themselves.

We're Going on a Bear Hunt, by Michael Rosen, illustrated by Helen Oxenbury (Walker). This is great for reading aloud as it has lots of repetition. Helen Oxenbury's illustrations show Dad and the kids in soft muted colours.

Books using rhyme to help with prediction

Each Peach, Pear Plum, by Allen & Janet Ahlberg (Puffin). These characters are ones that children have met in fairytales or nursery rhymes. After the first reading the child can predict the next character that will be introduced by the rhyme. Each page is almost an 'I spy' game as the reader hunts for the newly introduced character who is partly hidden somewhere in the delightful illustrations.

I'm Green and I'm Grumpy, by Alison Lester (Puffin). This is a great little book about dressing up. Half-pages are used to hide the next character dressed in fancy costume. By completing the rhyme, readers can guess what the child will be dressed up as next. A companion book is *Monsters are Knocking*.

Drummer Hoff, by Barbara Emberley, illustrated by Ed Emberley (Bodley Head). In this book with unusual illustrations a procession of military personnel bring the different parts needed to construct a cannon. It is Drummer Hoff who fires it. Repetition and rhyme encourage children to join in 'reading'.

Books with a cumulative pattern

Shoes from Grandpa, by Mem Fox, illustrated by Patricia Mullins (Ashton Scholastic). As this story develops young listeners soon join in. The pattern and rhyme, as well as the cumulative text, invite participation. The illustrations are in a wonderful collage.

The Gingerbread Man. This has been published in many different books. All are useful as they retain the structure of the little old woman, little old man and other characters, all chasing the gingerbread man.

The Great Big Enormous Turnip, by Alexei Tolstoy, illustrated by Helen Oxenbury (Picture Mammoth). The illustrations in this are a delight. Three-year-olds soon join in to help the old man, the old woman, the granddaughter, the dog, the cat and the mouse as they pull and pull and pull at the turnip.

The Very Hungry Caterpillar, by Eric Carle (Puffin). A small green grub eats its way through the week in this outstanding picture book that introduces number, days of the week and the butterfly's lifecycle.

There Was an Old Lady Who Swallowed a Fly. There are many versions of this story, all using the same repetition to build the story.

Children with Special Needs

❧

*A*s parents we know that all children have special needs – my child's needs may not be the same as your child's needs. In this chapter I use the term to refer to children who are hearing-impaired, have sight problems, are developmentally delayed, have an orthopaedic problem or have Down syndrome. All these children will benefit by sharing fingerplays, nursery rhymes, books and stories.

HEARING-IMPAIRED CHILDREN

Some points to keep in mind.

- Remember that the main reason for using stories and books with your child is enjoyment. Without enjoyment, the session becomes hard work for you and your child.

- Fingerplays, rhymes, stories and books have a major part to play in helping develop the language skills of these children.
- The more severe the hearing loss the more difficult it will be for children to make the connections necessary for understanding stories.
- Hearing impairment in some children is not diagnosed until the child is a toddler, leading to delay in language development.

Use the same materials as for hearing children but with the following modifications, considerations or adjustments.

- **Fingerplays.** These are used with hearing-impaired children for the same reasons that they are used with hearing children, but for hearing-impaired children language stimulation is even more important.
- **Nursery rhymes.** Introduce these along with fingerplays as oral games so that children can follow the rhythm of language. Tap out or clap a rhythm on the child's hand. Later introduce rhymes in books so that the child sees the illustration. Remember that hearing-impaired or profoundly deaf children need to look at the carer's face to 'hear'. The child cannot look at a book and at the speaker at the same time.

- **Board books.** When these are used to 'point and say', ensure the child is watching the adult's face as the word is said. Say the word clearly then show the illustration in a board book, ABC or counting book.

- **Wordless books.** Hearing-impaired children can follow the story just as hearing children can, but check their understanding by discussing the events in the story. For example, after sharing *Sunshine*, say 'Show me the little girl getting dressed. Show me the daddy and mummy'.

- **Flap books.** These are used just as for a hearing child but ensure the child understands. Ask 'What is Spot looking for? Where is Spot?'

- **First story books.** Read these as clearly as possible (but do not distort your normal speaking) to allow the child to make the most of their residual hearing. Check their understanding through questions or discussion.

- **Picture books.** For children with mild loss there should be no problem reading in a one-to-one situation in the home. However, when the child goes to childcare or kindergarten the teachers and carers must be told about even mild loss. Then they will ensure that the child is placed where they can hear best during story time.

If children have a moderate to severe loss you will need to check how much they have followed the story.

Hints for working with hearing-impaired preschoolers

- Children who wear hearing aids have trouble filtering out background noise from a speaking voice. Select a quiet area to read to the child. At home, avoid background noise such as noise from an airconditioner, radio, television or washing machine.
- Make sure that you have the child's attention before beginning to speak or read.
- Speak normally and at a normal volume.
- Allow the child ample time to respond to what you ask.
- Encourage the child to make the most of the visual clues. From the time they start to interact with picture books, encourage the child to use the illustrations to help in understanding the story.

CHILDREN WITH IMPAIRED SIGHT

The disability may range from minor vision impairment to blindness. Literature helps build language and listening skills in these children. It is also important in building concepts of objects within their environment. Listening skills are particularly important for these children, as much of their information at school will come via audio material.

Hints for working with sight-impaired preschoolers

- **Fingerplays.** Use these as for sighted children. Fingerplay is a valuable activity as it helps establish body awareness and show the rhythm of language.
- **Nursery rhymes.** As for sighted children. These help in developing language, listening and cognitive skills.
- **Board books.** May be used, but make sure that textures are included in showing shapes. This can be done by using any of the excellent commercial books that incorporate felt, fur and fabric. Ordinary board books can be adapted by outlining shapes with textured paint to raise the outline.
- **Stories.** Can be told or read to children. You might use real objects to set the mood of the story, such as a toy bear, plastic rabbit or model car.

- **Wordless picture books.** Place child's hand on
  the page and explain the action. For example, for *Sunshine*: 'This is a little girl asleep in bed. Now she
  is waking up. Here she is sitting up and reading her
  book. She is out of bed with her doll and her book.
  She is at the door of her mother and father's bedroom
  but she knows they are still asleep . . . '.
- **Picture books.** Read the story and describe the
  accompanying illustration. When explaining be
  explicit. For example, for *Where the Wild Things Are*:
  'Max is in his bedroom. He is standing by the bed
  and the door is shut'.

When children get past the toddler stage they can have
stories on tape. This will allow them to select their
favourite book just as their sighted peers do. Parents,
grandparents, aunts, uncles or friends can tape these stories to give a wide selection of stories and voices.
Commercial tapes are available for many children's
books.

Children with some sight can be encouraged to use it
to examine illustrations. Select books with large clear
illustrations and with large print on uncluttered pages.
Spot books have large print.

DOWN SYNDROME CHILDREN

Down syndrome children go through the same stages as other children, but later. In *Babies with Down Syndrome: A New Parents' Guide* by Karen Stray-Gunderson there is a table of information (on p. 126) which shows that 'normal' children crawl between six and eleven months, whereas Down syndrome babies crawl between seven and twenty-one months; 'normal' children walk between eight and eighteen months, and Down children between twelve and sixty-five months. Similar results are shown for other developmental milestones.

A report in the same book (p. 127) cites the positive results of an early intervention program for Down children undertaken at the University of Oregon. In some areas the children's development was the same as or ahead of 'normal' children. If this happens with such skills as feeding themselves or saying 'dada' or 'mama', then it follows that Down children must benefit from being introduced to fingerplays, nursery rhymes, stories and books with a caring adult. Since these activities help 'normal' children's language, social, physical, listening and cognitive skills, then they must help Down children who are passing through the same developmental stages.

Hints for working with Down syndrome children

- They may have short attention spans, so work in short time frames.
- The child may need many more repetitions before remembering a rhyme or game.
- They may need to have fingerplays and rhymes broken into smaller parts to help them remember.
- Make sure that the area is free of any distractions when reading with the child.
- Find and use the time of the day that is best for the children, when they are most co-operative.

CHILDREN WITH PHYSICAL DISABILITIES

- **Fingerplays.** Children with physical disabilities will benefit from being introduced to these. You may need to modify the movement depending on what the child enjoys. Fingerplays can help the child develop body awareness and fine motor skills.
- **Nursery rhymes.** These will help language development by giving the children a sense of language rhythm. Even if the children's physical development restricts their language they may still enjoy the sound of nursery rhymes.
- Introduce **board books** showing bright single

objects. This can be useful in developing the child's ability to focus, as well as helping with language.

- **Picture books** and **wordless books** will be useful for the child who is developing language. Children with physical problems may need help in handling books.
  - They may not be able to turn pages without assistance.
  - The size of a book is important for children in wheelchairs.
  - The weight of the book may be a problem for some children.
  - The pages must be sturdy enough to allow the child to turn them without tearing.
  - Books must be able to lie flat when they are opened.

Some children with special needs may have trouble understanding concepts that are not formed from concrete objects. For example, a deaf child and a Down child can see the difference between big/small and up/down, yet have difficulty understanding 'lonely', 'wicked' or 'cruel' – concepts that appear even in traditional or fairy stories aimed at very young children.

A Final Word

$\mathcal{T}$his book has focused on shared reading for babies and toddlers, but it is important that parents continue to read to children long after they can read for themselves. Karen D'Angelo Bromley, in *Language Arts: Exploring the Connections* (p. 138), reports on three studies that showed school-aged children who were read to every day made significant gains in vocabulary and comprehension compared with others who did not hear books read.

Apart from the gains in comprehension and vocab, I believe that reading to children as they go through school is important for a different reason. Parents who read to older children can introduce books that the new reader finds too difficult to tackle alone. If a young reader is struggling with a book that seems to have a slow start, it can be brought to life by an adult reader. Long before they can read for themselves children can be introduced to such classics as *Charlotte's Web*, *Storm Boy* or *The Lion, the Witch and the Wardrobe*.

As they grow up your children may not remember that you ironed their clothes to within an inch of their lives or dusted until the house shone – but they will not forget the times you shared a memorable book. They will remember how you laughed together over *Mr McGee and the Biting Flea* or cried together over *Jenny Angel* or *The Velveteen Rabbit*. I can still remember my Year 4 teacher reading us *Blinky Bill* and how we all cried when Mr Bear was shot.

Appendix:

Storybooks on Video

There are many excellent animated videos based on picture books. Some parents and teachers are concerned that watching these may lessen the value of the book, but I have found the opposite to be true. When I have used these I have adopted the following procedure.

I introduce the book first so that the child knows and enjoys the story and the characters. After the book has been read several times I introduce the video. The child already knows the story – the animation, voices and music add to their enjoyment. Don't be afraid that your child will become bored with it. Children sometimes demand to watch their favourites dozens of times before finding another favourite.

Note that these are all books that have been animated

to become videos, not videos or films that have subsequently been published as books. There is a great difference!

Adventures of Spot. This is the story of Spot, his mother Sally and father Sam. The video includes animated versions of seven Spot books. Each is quite short, to fit the attention span of young children.

Changes, Changes. This shows a wooden man and woman constructing a home from a group of blocks. They change their construction to a fire engine, then a boat and a train before finally remaking their house.

Corduroy. The story of Corduroy the toy bear, who is waiting in a store to find a loving home.

Doctor De Soto. This is the story of a dentist who is a mouse. Dr De Soto and his wife treat a fox with severe toothache. They then have to find a way to outfox him as he plans to eat them.

Five Bear Stories. This video has different stories that all feature bears: *Corduroy*, *Blueberries for Sal*, *The Bear and the Fly*, *Panama* and *Happy Birthday Moon*. Some are better known than others.

Gumdrop Makes a Start. The books about Gumdrop the car can be found in most libraries. This film shows Gumdrop when he was a new car, and follows his adventures over many years.

Hairy Maclary. This wonderful video has ten stories about Hairy Maclary, his doggy friends, sneaky Slinky Malinki and scary Scarface Claw. Great!

Kipper, the Seaside. Children may know Kipper from the books by Michael Inkpen. This video has four stories: *The Seaside, The Visitor, The Umbrella* and *Nothing Ever Happens.*

Old Bear and Friends. This is a set of three videos that retell the stories from Jane Hissey's books: *Old Bear, Little Bear's Trousers, Jolly Tall, Little Bear Lost* and *There Were Five in a Bed.*

Paddington Bakes a Cake. This has ten short stories about Paddington Bear.

Paddington Bear in Touch. This also contains ten animated stories of Paddington Bear.

Paddington Bear Video Show. This is another collection of ten stories involving Paddington Bear.

Peter Rabbit and Benjamin Bunny. This is a delightful video of stories about Peter and Benjamin's problems when they disobey their parents and visit Mr McGregor's garden.

Rosie's Walk and Other Stories. This is a family favourite in our house. Other books on the tape are *The Story about Ping, Charlie Needs a Cloak, Curious George* and *Norman the Doorman.*

Spot's First Video. This is great. It shows six of the well-known Spot books: *Spot's First Walk, Spot's Lost Bone, Spot's Surprise Parcel, Spot in the Woods, Spot's Birthday Party* and *Where's Spot?.*

The Owl and the Pussy Cat. This video has six well-known picture books by award-winning illustrators. In addition to the title book there are *Petunia, The Napping House, Peter's Chair, Changes, Changes* and *Make Way for Ducklings.*

The Snowman. This is a beautiful adaptation of Raymond Briggs' book about the friendship between a small boy and the snowman he creates.

Tom Kitten and Jemima Puddleduck. These two are taken from the Beatrix Potter books. The first shows Tom

Kitten and his sisters who have been dressed ready for visitors. But they manage to lose their clothes in the garden. *Jemima Puddleduck* shows how Jemima almost became the fox's dinner.

Where the Forest Meets the Sea. This shows the beauty of the rainforest through Jeannie Baker's beautiful collage. A truly lovely film.

Where the Wild Things Are. This is really great. Other stories by Maurice Sendak included on this tape are *Pierre, Chicken Soup with Rice, One was Johnnie* and *In the Night Kitchen.*